Discovering
County Durham

P.127

Discovering
County Durham

RON & MARLENE FREETHY

JOHN DONALD PUBLISHERS LTD
EDINBURGH

ISBN 0 85976 378 1

British Library Cataloguing in Publication Data
A catalogue record for this book is available from the British
Library.

Typeset by IMH (Cartrif), Loanhead, Scotland
Printed & bound in Great Britain by Bell & Bain Ltd., Glasgow

Introduction and Acknowledgements

Although County Durham suffered less than other counties during the reorganisation of the boundaries in 1974, it did have its borders altered and had bits pinched and given to South Tynedale and to Cleveland.

In our opinion geographical boundaries are always far better than those drawn up in the offices of ambitious politicians. In this book we have therefore written about old County Durham with its northern boundary delineated by the Tyne and the other borders marked by the Tees.

Our grandparents hailed from South Shields and although they have been long dead they would have refused to call themselves South Tynedalers - they were not from Durham either - they were proud to hail from County Durham.

The preparation of any travel book relies on other people as well as the diligence of the authors. We are grateful to Dudley Green, a dear friend and author of *Discovering Hadrian's Wall* in this series, with whom we discussed Roman settlements in Durham.

County Durham is a friendly place and this was reflected in the help given to us by curators and staff of such museums as Beamish, Darlington's Railway Museum, the Tanfield Railway, Killhope Wheel Lead Mining Centre and the Historic Ship Repair Centre at Hartlepool. The latter has such an impressive reputation that at the time of writing it is proposed that when the Royal yacht Britannia is retired in 1996 she will be berthed at Hartlepool.

All this suggests that the reputation of Durham as a dour industrial county is a gross slander. Most of its heavy industry has gone and to be honest we regret its passing because here hard work, beautiful buildings, glorious scenery and proud history have lived long in harmony.

As our readers use this book to discover the delights of County Durham they should forget the dour image, enjoy Durham city, stroll along its surprisingly clean rivers and spend time in its museums which lead the way in modern thinking.

We love Durham and hope that this shines through in the chapters which follow.

R. & M. F.

Contents

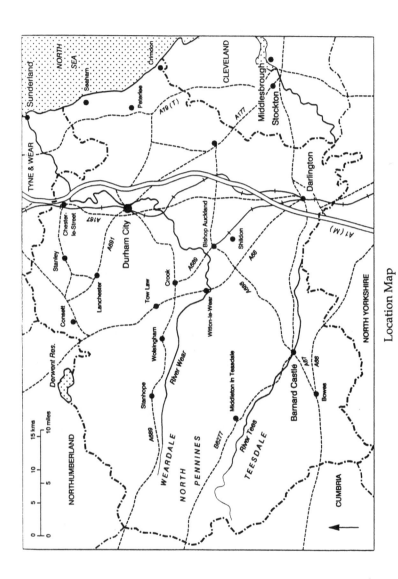

Location Map

viii

CHAPTER 1

County Durham–The Land of the Prince Bishops

Durham is unique in the sense that it is wrong even to refer to it as merely Durham. Lancashire, Cheshire, Somerset, Devon, Yorkshire or any other old county of England must be satisfied with one name but Durham has two and we must refer to it as County Durham. Here then we have a small county with a double name and a great history.

Here is the land of the Prince Bishops who ruled the County Palatine with both sword and mitre. In Norman England the area known as Northumbria was far removed from London but had a rich catchment from which armies could be recruited and paid for. Northumbria was still, however, remote and difficult to defend against the Scots. The English King needed someone he could trust, but he found it difficult to find a reliable baron. He therefore turned to the Church and gave to the Bishop of Durham what amounted to Regal powers. The people also trusted the bishop, because since the days of St Cuthbert in the 7th century, this office had commanded both love and trust. Thus the Normans and the natives were delighted to have a Prince Bishop - who, of course, had to be a Norman - to combine the rôles of churchman, politician, civil servant and soldier. This arrangement worked so well that it continued for around 800 years. It has recently been resurrected, in name only, by the Tourist Board. The land of the Prince Bishops is still well worth protecting and discovering.

Initially the Price Bishops' territory, known as the Palatinate, extended well beyond the borders of the present county and included some of North Yorkshire and substantial parts of what became Northumberland obviously including Holy Island. This area had to be administered just like a small independent country, which is exactly what it was. The Prince Bishop could raise his own army, levy taxes and mint coins to pay for their upkeep. He could create his own barons and generate further capital by granting markets

1

and fairs which paid tythes and rents for the privilege. Anyone who flouted the laws of the Prince Bishop could be tried, fined and even executed for treason. This was certainly absolute power and the question is 'Did it corrupt?' On the whole the answer is that it did not, at least when considered within the context of the period, but the Bishops during the 13th and 14th century were certainly not typical churchmen. The most interesting character was Prince Bishop Bek who led armies into the field against the Scots and wielded a sword with the best of them. The Middle Ages saw the peak of the Bishops' powers, but thereafter they gradually declined and in 1836 the area was finally handed back to the Crown. The Palatinate Courts, however, only ceased to function in 1971 and thereby ended one of the most fascinating periods of English history.

Modern County Durham became confined between the River Tyne in the north, with the Tees in the south and the North Sea forming the eastern border. Only to the west is the physical border not quite so obvious, but these wild upland areas fringing North Yorkshire and Cumbria are equally fascinating although very, very different. This western border, including Upper Teesdale and Upper Weardale, provided the Prince Bishops with valuable hunting territory and even more valuable mineral rights. These included lead and coal both of which later made County Durham an industrialised area, but without permanently depriving it of all of its natural beauty.

The heather-clad moors are the breeding ground for many insects including the Emperor moth and some interesting species of dragon and damselflies. These lay their eggs in the damp spots which are the catchment areas for Durham's substantial rivers. Breeding amphibians and reptiles also occur here including common frog and toad, adder, lizard and slowworm the last three often seen sunning themselves on exposed rocks and stone walls. The bird life is interesting rather than rich and includes red grouse, curlew, ring ousel, skylark, grey wagtail, meadow pipit and wheatear all of which breed plus occasional sightings of barn, short eared, little and tawny owl; rarities such as peregrine, merlin and hen harrier have also been sighted.

Durham Castle is now part of the university complex, but was built at the time when the Prince Bishops were all-powerful.

For those who are prepared to get up early in the morning several species of mammal can be seen including roe deer, fox, badger, stoat, weasel and on one occasion we saw a hedgehog swimming across the upper reaches of the Wear above Stanhope. On the same day we watched a kestrel feeding its young overflowing from its nest set in the ruins of Finchale Priory near Durham and in the close by Cocken Wood picnic area we found breeding jay, great spotted woodpecker and sparrow hawk. The flora of upper Teesdale is rightly famous not only throughout Britain but is known to botanists throughout the world. This will be described fully in Chapter 2.

Despite the picture of desolate pit villages painted by the too-often ill-informed media, Durham and its coastline, now partly absorbed into the new counties of Cleveland and Tyne and Wear, which are not recognised in the present book, has a great deal to offer.

Both the Wear and the Tees are fast flowing rivers and have gouged out their own Pennine Dales and the former has also scraped out the meander overlooked by a rocky peninsula on which stands the proud city of Durham itself. Between Sunderland and Teesmouth there is a plateau of magnesian limestone which has been gradually sliced into by the erosive action of small but fast flowing streams to produce what are known as coastal denes which are unique to this area.

The geology of Durham is broadly divisible into three zones. Firstly there is a substantial block of Permian limestone laid down some 300 million years ago. This runs along the coast but also extends inland and gets broader as you move from north to south. The central area is composed of carboniferous shales, coals and sandstones which have provided the region with its heavy industries for which it has became famous although some would say infamous. Whether folk like it or not there is no doubt that the old mining areas of County Durham have character and we love them. Thirdly the western dales are made up of mainly carboniferous limestone laid down about 370 million years ago. At this time the region was covered by a shallow sea, rich in shellfish and it is the calcium-rich shells of these creatures laid down layer upon layer, century after century, which formed the sedimentary limestone. During the Ice Ages, which came much later and finally retreated only about 10,000 years ago, deposits carried first by the glaciers and then by rivers of meltwater were deposited on top of the limestone. Erosion of these and the limestone beneath has produced a number of spectacular waterfalls which the region, now intent on attracting tourists, has sensibly exploited.

As more and more of its mines close increasing amounts of money are being spent on reclamation schemes and this is bound to appeal to tourists ever eager to discover the unique character of County Durham. Those with an interest in the countryside will find much on offer including walking, cycling, boating and angling whilst the sporting enthusiast will have welcomed Durham's entry into the County Cricket championship in 1992 and also a trip to the racecourse at Sedgefield. For the tough walker the fact that the Pennine

Way passes through Durham on its way from Edale in Derbyshire to Kirk Yetholme in Southern Scotland, will be of interest. We described some of this route in our companion volume *Discovering the Pennines*. There are also a number of well marked rambles which have been increased in recent years by the adaptation of many old railway lines which have been closed and are now overgrown with a fascinating tangle of vegetation. These routes have the advantage of being flat which makes them ideal for those with young children and for those who are not so sound in wind and limb as they used to be. Some of the routes are ideal for cyclists and mountain bikes can be hired from several places. The County Council have produced leaflets not only for walkers but also for cyclists and there are guided excursions for both.

It is possible, as we shall see later, to explore Durham city from the deck of a motor cruiser but for those who love sailing or wind surfing there is plenty of opportunity to improve the essential skills. Derwent Reservoir Sailing Club will allow visitors' boats to be launched providing they are of the right classes. Prior arrangements can be made by contacting Mrs M. Donaldson, Eastnor, Jesmond Park West, Newcastle-upon-Tyne, NE7 7BU. Selset reservoir can offer wind surfing and day sailing by arrangement with Northumbrian Water's Recreation Department, Abbey Road, Pity Me, Durham, DHl SE2. There is also wind surfing on offer at South Durham Windsurfing Centre, Bishopton Lake, Stockton, Cleveland. Here there is a licensed bar, shop, hire of equipment and tuition. Arrangements can be made by ringing Sedgefield 0740 31057. For those on holiday and wishing to enjoy a spot of gentle fishing will find much on offer as Northumbrian Water have eleven reservoirs which are stocked with fine brown and rainbow trout. Permits to fish using either worm or fly can be obtained either for a day or for the season from the Pity Me address listed above. There are also stretches on the Tees and the Wear which can be fished for salmon and trout providing the angler seeks permission and has the relevant licence.

Whilst the aim of this book has been to prove that Durham has a past and a present there is also a rosy future not least on the sports' field.

Whilst the 1992 County cricket season was not one of success for Durham the presence of Test cricketers such as Wayne Larkins and the indomitable Ian Botham ensured that the team was both welcome and noticed. The sum of seven million pounds is being invested in the riverside stadium at Chester-le-Street and this has been the source of much media speculation. Some writers seem to have forgotten that County Durham has a long and distinguished history in the Minor Counties' League being a founder member way back in 1895. Durham in their first season were joint champions with Norfolk and nine championships have been won in 1895, 1900, 1901, 1926, 1930, 1976, 1980, 1981 and 1984 the most of any county except Buckinghamshire who have won an equal number.

In Ice hockey Durham Wasps have carried the banner of the county with great distinction and Sunderland have also been good ambassadors on the soccer field. The miners, quarrymen, farmers and shipbuilders of the county have always worked hard because they had to and played hard because they wanted to and the pub darts' teams have been as well supported as in other parts of the country but in Durham and North Yorkshire they also play a game of out-door quoits. Some historians suggest that the Romans first brought the game into the area and it proved very suitable where there was a village green. It looks simple until you try it. The idea is to throw a disc of iron weighing more than five pounds from a wooden base a distance of 13 yards to drop on an upright pin. This takes skill and a well developed arm muscle!

Even more muscle and courage is required to take part in the Shrove Tuesday football match held at Sedgefield. The ball is made of leather just a bit larger than a cricket ball which is first passed through a hoop on the green and a goal is scored when it is passed through the hoop again. As many as 700 players take part in this free for all and mighty tough it is!

Quieter progress is being made to restore the coast of County Durham led as one might expect by the National Trust. The coal industry, both mining and transportation, once blackened many cliffs and most beaches, but dramatic improvements were made during the 1980s. Beacon Hill near Heddon is rich in both flora and fauna whilst Blackball Rocks Nature Reserve is close to the old coastal colliery village. Here is found the Castle Eden Argus butterfly which feeds on the common rock rose and other flowers thriving here include clover, vetch and trefoils whilst the rare sea spleenwort occurs. Such is the quality of the sea water these days that sea anemones thrive including Beadlet, Plumose and Sargartia. Birdwatchers seek out a permit for Blackball in the hope of finding wintering snow bunting and arctic skua on passage.

Despite its traditional heavy industries declining we found throughout the writing of this book nothing but optimism and good humour continuing to produce a county well worth discovering.

CHAPTER 2

Upper Teesdale

Ask anyone to name England's highest mountain and Scafell will spring to the lips of the vast majority; ask for our second highest peak and you will almost certainly receive a wrong answer; perhaps Helvelyn or Saddelback, but certainly not Cross Fell. This scaring mass does not have a memorable shape, but it still rises to 2930 feet (893 metres) and dominates the Northern Pennines. On its eastern slopes are generated two fascinating geographical features, the Helm wind and the River Tees.

We have felt the icy chill and awesome strength of the Helm wind on more occasions than we care to remember. It is some consolation to know what is happening from a scientific point of view but it does not make it feel any more comfortable when it is blowing with full fury. The name is thought to derive from the word Helmet and certainly Cross Fell seems to wear a cap of cloud just before the wind strikes. All that is known is that the Helm is 'Katabatic' which means that it drops from a height and strikes downwards with great force. Most authorities are agreed that the wind is produced because of the shape of the mountain as warm air rises up its slope to funnel into contact with cool air at the top. The mass then crashes back downhill to meet the warm air with often frightening results. No wonder that the mountain was once known as 'Fiends Fell' or the place of the devils. It is said that during the 7th century St Paulinus climbed the mountain to confront the fiends and the cross he placed on the summit changed the name of the place even though the wind was not tamed. There have been many descriptions of the Helm, many not printable but the historian Bulmer does a better job than most: 'Sometimes when the atmosphere is quite settled, hardly a cloud to be seen and not a breath of wind stirring, a small cloud appears on the summit, and extends itself to the North and South; the Helm is then said to be on, and in a few minutes the wind is blowing so violently as to break down trees, overturn stacks, occasionally blow a person from his horse or overturn a horse and cart.' A local farmer was much more blunt as he told us 'Yon Helm is a lazy wind, it gahs reet thru' yah instead o' ganging round?'

In this wild and windy spot the rainstorms are equally dramatic and it is here that the River Tees is born. The source is at Tees Head some 2,550 feet (777 metres) above sea level and from this point it journeys around 75 miles (120 km) to the North sea. During this journey its speeding waters gouge out a fascinating valley especially in the first two crashing miles when it falls 700 feet (215 metres). This valley attracts botanists who study the flowers typical of an alpine climate and which has changed little since the ice began to retreat some 12,000 years ago. It is only during the last 20 years that the value and vulnerability of this area has been appreciated and we can see just how close it came to total extinction.

In 1963 it was decided that a National Nature Reserve should be established and 8,600 acres (3,500 hectares) were so designated but full protection has only been given since 1970. This has focused attention on the unique flora and it is now under threat from thousands of often clumsy or perhaps innocent and uneducated feet especially between May and August when the flowers are at their best. Here growing in the damp swampy regions are carpets of marsh marigolds their gloriously shiny yellow blooms reflecting each ray of even the weakest of sunshine proving that here is a truly alpine species, one of the toughest, simplest and most primitive of our flowering plants, a member of the Ranunculus family. Rana refers to the common frog which is also found in substantial numbers in these high pastures. In the slightly drier areas the pale pink blooms of birds-eye primrose grow and look more beautiful and natural here than in any other area we know. Those who study Phytogeography - the distribution of plants - find Teesdale unique for the study of Arctic and Alpine plants because both types are found in Teesdale. No wonder the National Nature Reserve is full of late spring and early summer visitors in search of Alpine bistort, Alpine rue, Teesdale violet, plus more than

130 other species. Obviously plant distribution depends upon the underlying rocks and a study of the geology of upper Teesdale is essential.

The oldest rocks in Teesdale are the Silurian slates which are about 500 million years old and there was once a small industry hereabouts producing slate pencils used in schools before paper and pencil could be afforded. From a botanical point of view, however, it is the sandwiched layers of limestone, sandstone and shale, which is important. These formations date to the Carboniferous period which began around 350 million years ago. These produce distinctive soil types which then provide a variety of plant habitats. Much of Northumberland and County Durham is dominated by a rock called Whin Sill also known as quartz dolerite and is dark, fine-grained crystalline rock formed during volcanic activity. The molten magna squeezed its way between the layers of Carboniferous rocks, this activity taking place about 290 million years ago. The Whinstone is very hard and the different rates of erosion have led to interesting land forms including crashing waterfalls which are such a feature of Upper Teesdale. The effect of heat on some of the rocks of the area has produced almost unique rock types. Sandstone subjected to intense volcanic heat produced quartzites, and shales were forged into slates both of which can be seen in other areas, but in Teesdale the effect upon Melmerby Scar limestone produced a crystalline structure called 'sugar limestone' a crumbly rock which is easily weathered and can also be affected by heavy footsteps of botanising tourists. Sugar limestone is rich in lime and low in phosphorus and this provides the ideal habitat for rare plants especially the deep blue spring gentian. Here also grow thrift and sea plantain equally at home here as on an exposed beach. In addition the growth of plants and, of course the animals which feed upon them, depends a great deal upon climate and few areas in Britain have more precipitation (snow and rain) than Upper Teesdale.

In view of the delicately balanced ecosystem described above it is hard to imagine permission being given for the construction of a reservoir - and yet this did happen in the 1960s and 1970s despite strenuous objections. In the political climate of the 1990s Cow Green Reservoir would never have been suggested let alone constructed. Prior to the construction of Cow Green beginning in 1967 Upper Teesdale was just an area of rich swampland known as the Weel which was looked at by the greedy eyes of industrial Teesside which found existing supplies of water from the tributaries of the Tees inadequate. These were the Rivers Lune, its waters impounded into the reservoirs of Selset and Grassholme, and the Balder which supplied three reservoirs at Balderhead, Blackton and Hury. It was predictable that the main river would be sought after and Cow Green's eventual construction was inevitable within the climate of the time when the word conservation was little, if at all, understood. Despite the strenuous efforts of the Teesdale Defence Fund, Royal Assent was given to the Cow Green Reservoir Scheme on 22 March 1967. So the great upland lake was constructed, but like Kielder Water further north, the wildlife has proved unexpectedly resilient and a large colony of black headed gulls has settled in the area with the wildfowl counts increasing sufficiently to attract birdwatchers especially during the winter months. The reservoir covers 41 acres and holds 40,000 million litres. Its depth is 75 feet (23 metres) and in the winter such is the severity of the weather that the whole expanse can freeze over. The wave action on the banks of the reservoir caused erosion and in the dry summer of 1984 a Bronze Age farmstead was exposed.

There is one essential difference in the planning of 'modern' reservoirs and this is the provision of car parks and the marking out of walking trails. Cow Green car park is reached from the B6377 between Middleton-in-Teesdale and Alston. During the 1990s Durham County Council planned a Teesdale Way, a long distance footpath of more than 70 miles.

Before the reservoir Cauldron Snout waterfall must have been dramatic and it is still awesome in heavy rainfall. Now just below the reservoir the Cauldron cascade of eight steps falls along a length of 1200 feet (366 metres). We have followed the footpath during most seasons of the year and heard the terrifying roar following a wet March morning and the gentle whisper of a dry August afternoon beneath blue sky and the song of a soaring skylark. It is easy to see how the legend of the Singing Lady originated. This tells the story of a local lass who fell in love with a lead miner who decided to return to his wife and his distraught lover threw herself into the torrent. Her song is still heard among the bubbling water.

Just below Cauldron Snout the Tees is swelled by its tributary the Maize Beck, which until the boundary changes of 1974 marked the border of Cumberland, Yorkshire and County Durham. However impressive Cauldron Snout may be it must play second fiddle to Upper Teesdale's most famous attraction - High Force. It is still a most impressive waterfall and we can still remember what it was like before the completion of Cow Green reservoir in 1971 frightening in its noise and whipped white waters. There is a car park and an inn above the falls; the tree-lined footpath leading down can be followed on payment of a small fee which is used to maintain the track and to provide fences to prevent the over-eager from falling down into the steep valley of the Tees. Here among the atmosphere, made heavy by the spray, ferns grow in profusion including the lemon scented mountain, common polypody, common spleenwort, oak and beech fern. Among the trees are resident jay, sparrowhawk, tawny owl joined in summer by wood warbler, tree pipit, redstart and common sandpiper, the latter very much at home along the banks of the river.

A short drive downstream leads to the Visitors' Centre at Bowlees, an ideal spot to discover the history of the area and also Low Force and Wynch Bridge. Bowlees itself is situated on a tributary of the Tees, just past the village of Newbiggin. The site was developed by Durham County Council assisted by a grant from the Countryside Commission and there is plenty of space to enable bird watchers to observe dippers and grey wagtails along Flushiemere Beck. For those who like short walks there are three strolls which can be covered in a day using the car park and toilets as a base. There is a signed walk of just under half a mile to Summerhill Force, a lovely waterfall behind which is the extensive Gibson's cave. Although this is on private land belonging to the Raby estate, permission has been given for

Middleton-in-Teesdale is an attractive spot with a spacious green and good parking.

responsible walkers to use the area. Along the north bank of the Tees are two other pretty spots - Low Force waterfall and Wynch Bridge less than a mile from Bowlees. Although Low Force is not so famous as Cauldron Snout or High Force it has its own unique attraction and Wynch Bridge, built in 1704 is probably the earliest suspension bridge in Europe. At Bowlees a Visitors' Centre has been set up in a converted chapel and has displays on the geology, history and natural history of the area. There is a shop and refreshments are available on site. Bowlees provides information on the nearby hamlet of Holwick once a busy lead mining area but now a quiet backwater.

Although there is an increasing number of bed and breakfast establishments those wishing to spend some time discovering Upper Teesdale may prefer to base themselves at Middleton-in-Teesdale or at 'Barney' as the locals affectionately call Barnard Castle.

The Bainbridge fountain in the centre of Middleton-in-Teesdale.

One of our favourite routes into Middleton-in-Teesdale is from Cumbria by following the signs from first Kirkby Stephen and then from Brough. The undulating road crosses rough open moorland and almost as soon as the border is crossed into Durham the colour of the moorland changes. We then look out for a sign indicating a picnic site to the right and at a distance of about four miles. This narrow road leads to one of Durham's hidden secrets. After passing Selset reservoir there is a small picnic site alongside Grassholme reservoir which in winter is an excellent place to do a sheltered spot of bird watching. The area, however, is at its best in May when we choose to park above the two reservoirs in front of a developing conifer plantation which serves also as the catchment area for two additional reservoirs close to Balderhead on the moor. Here we listen to skylarks and pheasants whilst watching oyster catchers displaying in preparation for breeding. In the last 20 years oyster catchers have changed their habits somewhat from being seabirds breeding solely on the coast. Possibly in response to excessive disturbance on their traditional shingle beaches they have moved up the rivers seeking out patches of river pebbles. Likewise they have proved adaptable with regard to diet and feed on the insects found amongst the cow pats and sheep droppings. Nothing is wasted in Nature's food chain. First time visitors are often confused by the occasional clap of thunder even on beautiful sunlit days, but this is not Nature's arsenal but the army on their nearby practice range.

Middleton-in-Teesdale, like many small towns in County Durham, began as an agricultural settlement later evolving into a market town, later swamped by industry and now striving gamely to return to agriculture and flirt seriously with tourism. Middleton is coping very well and is ideally situated to become a holiday resort. Those who love the wildlife of breezy moorlands will love it and so will those who enjoy industrial archaeology.

Middleton's broad and grassy centre is overlooked by old coaching inns and at the time of the cattle market it looks as rural as it was initially, probably as far back as Norman times. The effects of the presence of the Quaker-dominated London Lead Company is just but only just beginning to fade. The company arrived in 1815 and for almost a century ruled the town, but compared with the standards of the period proved to be benevolent employers. They were the first company in Britain to introduce a five day week and encouraged the miners to set up small holdings which ensured a much healthier diet than was normal in the industry where strength and stamina were vital. From Monday to Friday the men lived on site crowded together in grubby billets called shops. A sample of such a 'shop' can be seen at the Killhope Mining

Museum at the head of Weardale and described in chapter 4. The company also constructed impressive buildings and Middleton House was built for the superintendent and in the adjacent yard is a most impressive clock tower. Mastermen Place was built for the workers, yet another example of the employers' feeling for their staff and what is now the Trustee Saving Bank was initially the Teesdale Workmens' Corn Association which is said to be the world's first effort at constructing a co-operative store. Obviously the workers appreciated their bosses and in the square is the Bainbridge drinking fountain, a cast iron memorial built in 1877 in memory of a respected superintendent.

The church is also in context and was built in the 19th century, although it probably replaced a Norman building. Quakers were always tolerant to other peoples' religious views and Town End chapel to the east of the centre is another example of solid Victorian architecture. Given time such structures will be judged much more sympathetically than at present. A building which is certainly not in context is Greta Lodge situated just behind the church. It is a prefabricated building brought from Norway as part of the 1851 Great Exhibition held in London. From there it was for some reason brought to Middleton.

Between Middleton-in-Teesdale and Barnard Castle are a number of charming hamlets including Eggleston, Mickleton, Romaldkirk and Catherstone. These are quiet, sheltered spots and ideal bases from which walkers can head out onto the wild open moorlands. At Eggleston there is an attractive packhorse bridge, dating to the 17th century, crossing a clear stream which is a tributary to the Tees. This is the haunt of both pied and grey wagtail whilst further upstream are breeding dippers. There is a Victorian church which was built as a replacement for an earlier building which can still be seen in the grounds of Eggleston Hall, a 19th century gentleman's house, which is not open to the public.

Mickleton stands high above the south bank of the Tees and although it is now a long line of stone cottages there has been a settlement here since Neolithic times. The next village downstream is Romaldkirk but the most enjoyable route is

There has been a church at Romaldkirk since Saxon times, although the tower of the present building is 15th century.

to take a circular route threading among the complex of reservoirs including Grassholme, Selset, Balderhead, Blackton and Hury and then along the River Balder which is a tributary of the Tees. Our first visit to Romaldkirk was many years ago after an August thunderstorm followed by a rainbow and hot sunshine. The village with its complex of little greens and cottages with colourful flowers dripping with sparkling droplets looked enchanting. There has been a church here since Saxon times and there is documentary evidence that it had been destroyed before 1086. The village takes its name from St Rumwold who built the church in Anglo-Saxon times. Durham is full of churches of ancient origin, and it is no wonder that the Prince Bishops wielded such power and had so much influence. Romaldkirk's church is so impressive that it is easy to understand why it is often referred to as the Cathedral of the Dale. The nave and north aisle were constructed around 1155 and the arcade and transept around 1240. The chancel and vestry were rebuilt between 1360 and 1370 but the age of the structures they replaced is not known. The solid tower is 15th century.

Romaldkirk has not just one village green but several, each being equally charming.

Inside the church the most impressive piece of 'furniture' is the effigy at the end of the north transept. It is of special interest because it shows a knight dressed in full chain mail. Hugh Fitz Henry, the lord of Bedale, Ravensworth and Cotherstone was a renowned soldier. He was getting on in years when he was wounded in 1305 fighting in Scotland for Edward I546. He was transported to Barwick-on-Tees near Darlington but on March 12 he succumbed to his wounds. It was customary for the family to be buried at Jervaulx abbey in Wensleydale, but he expressed a wish to be remembered at Romaldkirk which had been granted to his relatives sometime between 1070 and 1086 by William of Normandy himself.

Such a fine church deserves a magical setting and Romaldkirk is just that with its haphazard arrangement of stone cottages, little alleyways and well kept greens. These are still cut and maintained at the expense of the church rector although there are discretely camouflaged collection boxes on some of the greens. The Rectory itself is a fine example of Georgian architecture.

Cotherstone is just as pretty and it is here that the River Balder joins the Tees both of which are surrounded by rich rolling pasture used as good grazing for cattle. It is here that the soft crumbly Cotherstone cheese is made and which can be purchased locally. At one time there was a castle here which although powerful in the 12th century is now little more than a few stones perched on the crown of a small mound. The church is an unremarkable Victorian structure but from it there is an attractive path which once led to the now closed railway station. Beyond this is one of the finest routes onto the moors which is very popular with picnickers during the summer. What better than this scenery drunk in whilst feasting on fresh bread, farm butter and Cotherstone cheese. For those who prefer bar snacks, the Fox and Hounds is an ideal retreat.

If Romaldkirk and Cotherstone are gems among the list of Teesdale villages, then Barnard Castle must be the most prized jewel among the towns of the river. On a gentle August morning we arrived at a small picnic site on the banks of the Tees near the bridge and looked up at the castle. The river, brown and full almost to bursting after almost a week of heavy rain crashed against the cutwaters of the bridge and we looked up at the people winding their way up the footpath to the town from the bridge. Such a wonderful castle is bound to have a fascinating history and no visitor, whatever the weather, can fail to be impressed. Whatever the day or the season the town centre close to the castle will be busy and parking is usually a problem for those who are not prepared to walk from the designated areas on the outskirts. The problems are even worse on the Wednesday market day.

Any discovery of the town should begin at the castle which gave it its name, although to the locals it will always be known as Barney. The castle is open on most days of the year, has a modest entry fee, holds occasional medieval pageants and is maintained by English Heritage to their usual excellent standard.

The castle commands a wonderful view of the medieval bridge over the Tees built on the site of a former ford, and was one of the most dominating in Norman England. The present building dates to 1125 and was built by Bernard

The Old Town Hall at Barnard Castle later became the butter market. It was photographed in the 1890s. To the left is the tower of the parish church of St. Mary. The street, appropriately called 'The Bank' can be seen descending in the background and leads to the River Tees.

Balliol and thus the correct name, still used in some guide books, should be Bernard's Castle. The family had just the right connections because Guy de Balliol fought alongside William at Hastings and along with other faithful followers he was rewarded with vast areas of land wrenched from the Saxons. Guy was given much of what is now Teesdale. John Balliol was for a short time King of Scotland until he made the error of betraying Edward I (1272-1307) who was a ferocious fighter and earned his nickname of the Hammer of the Scots. Once he had defeated Balliol, Edward confiscated his lands and gave them to the Earls of Warwick and as they eventually married and produced a Royal line Barnard's Castle passed to the Crown. In the 15th century Warwick the Kingmaker's daughter married the future Richard III and his emblem which is wild boar can be seen among the decorations on the wall of the Great Chamber. In 1569 the castle held out for eleven days of siege in support of Queen Elizabeth in what became known as the Rising of the Northern Earls in support of Mary Queen of Scots and the Catholic faith. Although the castle fell into ruin after this sufficient remains to show what an impressive building it

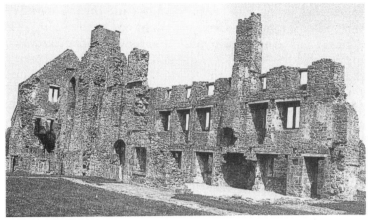

Egglestone Abbey is set in a pretty valley and its masonry often helps to focus the sound of bird song.

once was. The Round Tower is particularly fine and dates to the 13th and 14th centuries and the curtain walls, ramparts and the lines of the old moats can all be seen. In about 1630 Sir Henry Vane ordered the castle to be dismantled.

Outside the castle which occupies the crest of the hill above and overlooking the river, the town spreads out, making use of every inch of space with the butter market standing at the junction of the market with Thorngate and Newgate. To the left is the parish church and beyond this is the Bowes Museum whilst straight ahead from the butter market is a street called the Bank which leads steeply down to the river.

The parish church of St Mary looks plain and rather modern, but the interior clearly shows its Norman origins, although it was much altered during the period of the town's 19th century opulence. Within the rather dim interior the history of the families associated with the castle shine out from the darkness.

The town, despite its almost continual hustle and bustle, has many quiet and beautiful corners whilst some of its buildings are worth a long lingering look. Some of them are built from stone taken from the dismantled castle. Blagraves House was, in the 16th century, an inn and during the Civil War Oliver Cromwell spent the night of October 28th 1648 within it. Sufficient inns remain to satisfy both the hardened drinker and the historian. One can imagine what a roaring trade they did during the Turnpike era when the square would have echoed to the strident notes of the coaching horn. The Golden Lion dates to 1679 the Three Horseshoes to 1691 whilst the King's Head Hotel is also 17th century and may pre-date both the others. This was the base chosen by Dickens when he was researching *Nicholas Nickleby* basing the infamous Dotheboys Hall School at Bowes which will be described later in the chapter. Dickens would still recognise the market cross built in 1747 as the Town Hall but subsequently used as a butter market. Some time ago a friend gave us a photograph of the cross taken about 1890 and it has changed hardly at all since.

Descending the Bank leads to the ancient County Bridge which was, as its name implies, the old boundary between Yorkshire and Durham. There is a record of the bridge being repaired following the siege of the castle during the Rising of the North and so it must have existed long before this date. This is not surprising as the crossing here was of vital im-portance. There have been many alterations since but the basic medieval structure can still be recognised. It is possible to return to the town centre after visiting another ancient hostelry The White Swan Inn and via Thorngate to the Bank and the market cross. Time should be spent here to search out a plaque on the site of a shop owned by Thomas Humphreys. Although less well known than *Nicholas Nickleby*, *Master Humphrey's Clock* is a rattling good short story — Vintage Dickens!

Two interesting buildings close to Barnard Castle cause much confusion among first time visitors. Egglestone Abbey is nowhere near the village of a similar name but without the end 'e' and the Bowes museum is in Barnard Castle and nowhere near the ancient settlement of Bowes which is on the opposite side of the River Tees, but still in Durham.

Egglestone Abbey is open the year round, maintained by English Heritage, and entry is free. The site is magnificent

The Bowes museum brings a touch of France to Teesdale.

at the junction of Thorsgill Beck (a Scandinavian name) with the River Tees. The view of the abbey from the road out of Barnard Castle is magnificent. The building was begun by the Premostratensian Canons and a surprising amount remains. The cruciform church is easily recognisable especially the nave and chancel. The abbey was begun in 1195 with the White Canons led by Ralph Nulton. Egglestone was dissolved in 1540.

Bowes Museum looks as if a large chunk of 18th century France has been lifted stone by stone and dropped in Teesdale. The French connection is no accident as the house was designed by the French architect Jules Pellachet for George Bowes and his French actress wife who was named Josephine Benoite. Josephine's father was a clock maker and this explains the vast collection of timepieces and clockwork automatons including a silver swan made before 1774 and which still works. There is a 17th century 'lion clock' with swivelling eyes. George was rich thanks to the profits from his father's coal mines. The 10th Earl of Strathmore also made money from rents from his vast estates. The foundation stone was laid in 1869 but before it was complete Mrs Bowes died and at Bowes according to her wishes George opened the

Bowes Castle, with the church beyond it. The old moat can clearly be seen in the foreground. ˙

house as a museum in 1892. It is now administered by Durham County Council and it is hard to imagine a more beautiful museum in such a magnificent setting. It is open daily except Christmas and New Year and there is an entry fee. The park is always open and in summer there is a pleasant little cafe. In the grounds there are some magnificent trees including a huge monkey puzzle tree. Inside is a vast array of furniture, ceramics, tapestries and a famous art collection including works by Goya, El Greco and Canaletto. There is a table which once belonged to Marie Antoinette. It is, however, the building itself which takes the breath away.

Bowes village is situated off the A66 just to the south west of Barnard Castle. It developed because it stood at the entrance to the Stainmore Gap which has been a major route between the east and west of England for thousands of years. This explains why the impressive castle was built and like many parts of Teesdale had close associations with the Bowes Lyon family whose most famous member is the Queen Mother.

The Romans found it necessary to cross the Stainmore gap and built a road guarded by the forts at Stainmore, Bowes and Greta Bridge. Bowes was known as Lavatrae and compared to some its 4 acres (12 hectares) was quite small but still large enough to take up the ground now occupied by the ruins of the Norman Castle, the adjoining church and the vicarage. Apart from the fort there was also a bathhouse although all trace of this has long gone. County Durham does, however, have the most complete bathhouse to be found in Britain and which is being excavated at Binchester near Bishop Aukland to be described in chapter 4. Bowes, however, had the distinction of being the last outpost to be deserted at the decline of the Empire during the 4th century AD. This suggest that it was covering the retreat along an important road.

The route over Stainmore remained vital to the Anglo Saxons, to the Vikings and the Normans were soon aware of the strategic importance of Bowes and built a castle and later a church on the Roman site making use of the ready supply of cut stone.

Soon after the conquest William granted extensive lands to Alan Nigar the Earl of Richmond who initially built a simple castle to prevent marauding Scots passing through Stainmore. In 1170 a unique structure was constructed being only a keep of three storeys surrounded by a ditch but having no other associated building. Local folklore, which may have some basis in fact, suggests that the Earl of Richmond gave Bowes into the charge of his brother William supported by 500 archers. This worthy became known as William de Arcubus which was later shortened to Bowes - William the Bowman so to speak.

It is further suggested that William was an ancestor of the Bowes family of Streatlam who gave rise to the Earls of Strathmore and ultimately Elizabeth Bowes Lyon, the Queen Mother.

Being set in such an important position Bowes Castle was frequently raided by the Scots and by 1340 it was in such a sad state of repair that it was abandoned. The site is maintained by English Heritage and access if free. In a much better state of repair is the church of St Giles which although contemporary with the castle and containing Roman stonework has been much altered. In the churchyard is the grave of a ferocious schoolmaster and also some of his unfortunate pupils. The wicked man was called William Shaw and Charles Dickens used the initials W.S. and created the character of Whackford Squeers. His academy which Dickens called Dotheboys Hall is now a collection of dwellings at the west end of the village and the old pump used by the school can still be seen.

Stainmore continued to be an important east-west route through the Pennines throughout the stage coach era and the Unicorn Inn which still stands did a roaring trade. On Wednesday 31st January 1838 Charles Dickens was in the area and notebook at the ready gave William Shaw an infamous place in literary history. It is even said that the character of Smike was based on a pupil named George Taylor who ran away from the school only to perish of exposure after a period on the hills. George is also buried in the churchyard.

Dickens based himself at Barnard Castle and so too must the modern day discoverer of Teesdale. Before following the Tees towards Piercebridge there are several other places which should not be missed including Staindrop, Raby Castle and Cockfield and yet another fine building at Rokeby.

Staindrop, set on Langley Beck yet another of the tributaries of the Tees, consists of a series of greens, a church and a collection of mainly 18th century stone houses. In 1971 it was designated a Conservation Area, but a tour of the large village should wait until Raby Castle has been visited because it was this wonderful place which has long controlled the fortunes of Staindrop. Raby Castle usually opens at Easter and then in May and June on Wednesdays and Sundays and on Bank Holidays. From July to September it opens daily except Saturdays. The park and gardens open between 11 am and 5.30 pm and the castle from 1 pm to 5 pm. There is an entry fee, plenty of parking, picnic tables, a souvenir shop and a cafe situated in the old stables.

Raby Castle is set in a 200 acre (80 hectares) park which has been the well cared for home of Lord Barnard's family for more than 350 years, but the castle is even older. It was mainly built in the 14th century by the initially powerful Neville family who finally overplayed their hand by joining the followers of Catholic Mary of Scots against Protestant Elizabeth in the 1569 Rising of the North. It was first seized by the Crown and later purchased by the Vane family from whom the present Lord Barnard is descended.

At one stage in their history the Vanes almost lost the estate for a similar misjudgement to that made earlier by the Nevilles. Henry Vane supported Parliament during the Civil War and even though he opposed the execution of Charles I he did not escape retribution at the Restoration of 1660. He was executed at the Tower of London, but the estate remained in the family who sensibly kept a low profile for a while.

This has been a home and consequently much altered during the 18th and 19th centuries but not all the medieval features were removed and the Great Kitchen is 600 years old. The Baron's Hall is a treasure house and there is fine furniture of all periods, delicate china and paintings including the work of Reynolds and other masters. The entrance is imposing and large enough to allow carriages to be driven through it and out via the back door beneath the Chapel Tower. Anyone wishing to know the size of a carriage should visit the coach house outside which is a collection of horse-drawn vehicles once used by the Barnard family. The large walled gardens have been carefully nurtured and the modern developments have not disturbed either the ancient yew hedges or the fig tree which is 200 years old. The deer in the park are worth a visit for their own sake.

As you would expect of one so close to a great house St Mary's church is among the most impressive in County Durham. It dates back to the 8th century and traces of Saxon windows and also the old roof line can still be seen. As one would expect of the local place of worship of first the Nevilles and then the Vanes who became Lord Barnards, the church has been enlarged and altered in almost every century from early Norman times onwards. The Nevilles's influence can be seen not only in their oak, alabaster and marble effigies but also for their gift of the magnificently ornate pre-Reformation screen. This is the only such screen in the whole of the county. There are few churches in England which can boast a better or larger collection of effigies than St Mary's. In 1850 an overflow mausoleum had to be built. Beneath the floor of the church is the now redundant water engine which once pumped the now electrically driven organ.

The village itself, as well as the church, has a well cared for look about it as does most of the property of the Raby estate. This is extensive enough to include other parts of Teesdale including High Force waterfall.

Nearby is the village of Cockfield which was the home of the remarkable Dixon family who descended from the 17th century steward of Raby Castle. George Dixon was born in 1731 and being a wealthy colliery owner was able to indulge his hobbies of engineering and chemistry. It was he who discovered coal gas and his brother Jerimiah became even more famous. He was a very skilled astronomer and surveyor who with his friend Charles Mason surveyed around Maryland and Pennsylvania in the United States. Who these days has not heard of the Mason-Dixon Line? As lovers of Dixieland jazz we think of Dixon of Cockfield every time we listen to a disc. The Dixons continued to be influential as we discovered as we were preparing another of this series of volumes *Discovering the River Thames*. Whilst looking at Cleopatra's Needle on London's Embankment we discovered that it was brought to England in 1878 by another Teesdale-bred George Dixon!

Cockfield was settled prior to Norman times and has retained many of its ancient rights. The Fell is a common land in every sense of the word with villagers still having the right to graze cattle, collect firewood, cut stone or dig coal. Fell Reeves are still ceremoniously appointed to ensure that nobody gets greedy and it is still possible to see bell-shaped depressions from which 'open cast' coal was removed centuries ago.

Three miles to the south east of Barnard Castle is Rokeby, yet another fascinating house and built in 1735 by the amateur architect 'Long Sir Tom'. Sir Thomas Robinson built the house in an extravagant Palladian style and now with its enclosed park it has settled into the Teesdale countryside remarkably well. To the east of the present house is the ruin of the 14th century Northam Tower which originally belonged to the Rokeby family and from which the estate takes its name. The Rokebys had to sell their estate after backing the Royalists during the Civil War and after a series of owners including Long Sir Tom, the estate was bought by the Marritt family. This was in 1769 and they have been loving tenants ever since. They were visited in 1809, 1812 and 1813 by Sir Walter Scott and it was here that he wrote his long romantic poem *Rokeby*. Since the 1980s the hall has been open to the public. It is as well to check the times of opening with the Tourist Information Office in Barnard Castle. It is usually open on Monday and Tuesday between May and September. It is worthwhile making a special effort to see this gem from the inside as on display is a collection of needlework by Anne Marritt (1726-97). Many paintings are on display although Valazquez's *Rokeby Venus* is now in the National Gallery in London. What a pity! But never mind; the reproduction at Rokeby still looks good. The grounds are magnificent and a walk leads to Scott's Cave and the 'Meeting of the Waters' where the River Tees is joined by yet another substantial tributary, the Greta.

Not far from Rokeby is Whorlton Lido, a 14 acre park four miles from Barnard Castle on the south bank of the Tees. This offers lots of fun for children including a 15 inch gauge steam railway. It is close to a suspension bridge built across the Tees in 1829 and the village of Whorlton itself is neat and colourful and situated on the north bank of the river. The village is mentioned in documents dating from as early as 1050 when it was known as Queorningtun and St Mary's church has a Saxon foundation although it was rebuilt in 1853.

From Barnard Castle the Tees wends its still unpolluted way to Piercebridge via the attractive villages of Winston and Gainford which are two of the rivals to be considered as the most attractive villages in County Durham. Winston is yet another Teesdale village built high on the banks of the river and surrounded by trees including alder and willow. Spanning the river is a 111 foot single span stone bridge which when it was constructed in 1764 was the largest of its kind in Europe. Although the church of St Andrew was

The remains of the Roman bridge at Piercebridge once spanned an important crossing before the River Tees changed its course.

insensitively restored in the 19th century sufficient remains of the 13th century furnishings to make it worth exploring. The font, for example, is unusual in showing dragons fighting. The memorials in the nave are a source of wonder to brass rubbers especially that dedicated to Aaron Arrowsmith (1750-1823) who in his day was well known as a cartographer. How strange that he should be born so close to Dixon of Cockfield.

If Winston is attractive then Gainford is beautiful being built around a two layered village green and the potentially damaging A67 road from Barnard Castle to Darlington has worked to its advantage. Modern development has been allowed on one side of the road and the ancient village left on its own in splendid isolation on the other. The church is of particular interest having Saxon origins with the original stones being taken from the Roman fort at nearby Piercebridge. Although it is Early English in style it is actually on the site of a Saxon monastery. As at Staindrop the memorials in the church are its best feature, this time relating to the Middleton family who lived at Gainford Hall which is an imposing Jacobean residence but not open to the public. The house is very reminiscent of Hardwick Hall in Derbyshire which is said to have more areas of glass windows than stone walls. This was a real sign of opulence in the days when glass was a luxury.

Those who wish to discover a little known feature of Gainford should slip on a pair of boots or better still wellingtons and follow a path upstream along the Tees for about a mile. Our sense of smell told us when we were approaching the sulphur springs which during the 19th century were popular with those who enjoyed punishing themselves by drinking the waters. Gainford Spa almost but not quite, became a rival to Harrogate and Scarborough in Yorkshire and Buxton in Derbyshire.

Our first introduction to Piercebridge was accidental and underlined our belief in the friendliness of village folk. On a Bank Holiday we had struggled to persuade an elderly car to carry us down Teesdale despite a leaking radiator. At Piercebridge she finally boiled and we watched steam issue from all parts of the system. Within minutes cottage doors opened, jugs of water, pots of tea and tins of Radweld and other sealants appeared as if by magic. We were almost ready for off when we noticed the sign to the Roman Fort and decided to explore. First we had a meal at the George Hotel on the old Yorkshire side of the river. We found that it was not only our car which stopped short in Piercebridge, but so did a Grandfather clock. Displayed in the Inn is the clock which stopped when its owner died. The event was celebrated by Henry Works's song *My Grandfather's Clock* which 'stopped short, never to go again when the old man died?'

The Roman fort and the bridge further downstream deserve to be listed more frequently in the places of interest

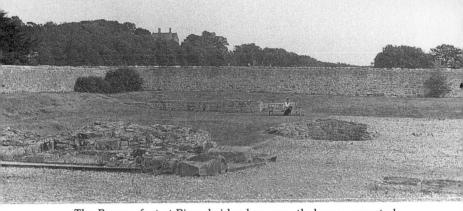

The Roman fort at Piercebridge has recently been excavated.

for tourists. Like Binchester described in chapter 4, Piercebridge fort protected an important point at which Dere Street which ran from York to Hadrian's Wall crossed the Tees. We feel that a museum should be set up here but already many of the important artefacts have been removed either to the British Museum or other impersonal establishments in the North East of England.

The main focus of the fort now lies beneath the attractive village green but there are extensive excavations signed just off it. It is freely open at all times and among the tangle of stones are a number of wooden seats. At the entrance is an Information Board giving details of the fort's history and subsequent uncovering. Some historians have suggested that the Romans may have operated a sort of canal system enabling them to use this and the River Tees to transport goods. This would have improved the transport of heavy goods in areas where Dere Street followed the steep contours of hills. There is no doubt that there was an important bridge here and the ruins of this can be reached by following a well marked short footpath from just beyond the George Hotel. Strictly speaking the bridge is on the Yorkshire side of the Tees which here forms the county boundary. The presence of the bridge on dry land proves that since Roman times the river has changed its course. The remains have been very skilfully excavated following its accidental discovery during excavations for river gravel and quarrying for stone. One pier of the bridge has been uncovered almost in mint condition after lying protected by a layer of silt for around two thousand years and the zig-zag arrangement of stones to break up the force of the water striking the bridge supports can clearly be seen. If the river changed course again it seems that only minor repairs would be needed for the bridge which would have been made partly of wood, to be once more functional.

From Piercebridge onwards to the sea at Darlington the Tees becomes ever more industrial. This lower section and the estuary are described in Chapter 3.

Teesdale had its very own poet Richard Watson (1833-1891) who wrote:-

I've wandered many a weary mile,
And in strange countries been;
I've dwelt in towns and on wild moors
And curious sights I've seen.
But still my heart clings to the dale
Where Tees rolls to the sea,
Compared with what I've seen I'll say
The Teesdale hills for me.

CHAPTER 3

Darlington and Stockton-on-Tees

Darlington was originally a Saxon town established on the banks of the River Skerne a tributary of the Tees. The present church dedicated to St. Cuthbert is probably of Saxon origin and may even have been erected on the site of a pagan burial ground. Historians regard St. Cuthbert's as one of the most important early English churches in Britain, mainly because very few additions or alterations were made after 1250. It is a delightfully graceful building set on a gently sloping green right in the centre of town. The graveyard is shaded by trees, planted with colourful flowers and provided with seats. Locals and visitors use the area as a quiet park and it is hard to imagine that those laid to rest here would object to the company. We once shared a packet of crisps and a juicy plum with a couple of grey squirrels whilst watching a blackbird carry food to her young in this town churchyard which feels as if it was set right in the heart of the countryside.

Immediately outside the gates is the large market square. Both church and market were an important part of the interests of the Bishopric of Durham, and it was this which persuaded Bishop Pudsay to construct a complex of buildings to reflect his importance. By 1180 Pudsay had erected his own palace on the site of the present town hall - indeed it probably carried out the same function. St. Cuthbert's itself was more of a cathedral than a standard parish church and it had a chantry in which teaching was an integral part and from the building three other parishes were governed - Blackwell, Cockerton and Archdeacon Newton. The present church still has four Church wardens, a most unusual feature. Two officials act for Darlington, one for Archdeacon Newton and one for the two manors Blackwell and Cockerton. The parish guide book on sale in the church points out that the austerity of the church furnishings is due to the fact that the Bishops of Durham allowed no other Lord of the Manor to exercise rights here, and so there was no

Darlington's parish church, dedicated to St Cuthbert, is a quiet haven in the middle of a busy but pleasantly situated town.

gentry to give money to St Cuthbert's. It therefore lacks monuments, side chapels, effigies or other ornamentation. The church and the lucrative market associated with it in the early days was governed by a faceless bailiff employed by the Prince Bishop of Durham and who had, therefore, no permanent roots. Despite this there is plenty of interest within the building including the figure of St. Cuthbert whose body is said to have rested at Darlington as it was carried from Lindisfarne to keep it from the despoiling hands of the Danes prior to finding its permanent resting place in Durham. St. Cuthbert is depicted holding the head of King Oswald who in the 9th century did so much to ensure that Northumbria remained Christian. Eventually even the Danes were converted and in the north transept is a fragment of a Danish hog-back tombstone. This would seem to have shown a long horse with a muzzled bear's head facing inward at each end. The ridge of the horse's back and the bear's head can both clearly be seen on the much eroded stone. In the south transept there are the worn remains of two piscinae, or sinks, in which the vessels used in the mass were washed. These were not used after the Reformation, but the fact that there were two proves that there was once two altars. For many centuries a school was held in the north chancel. St. Cuthbert's kept an interest in education until 1874, either within the church itself or in a building once sited in the churchyard. The tablet from the last school is now incorporated into the south eastern gateway.

No one interested in church architecture can fail to be impressed by the 72 foot long nave with soaring columns showing quite unusual workmanship considering that it was built in the 13th century and has not been altered since. Close to one of these columns are a few fragments of pre-Norman crosses and thus establishes the site as an early focus of Christianity.

One further question must be asked regarding the lack of gentry in and around Darlington - why did such a group not develop after the influence of the Prince Bishops waned? The answer is that the influence of the Quakers developed quickly and it was they who placed Darlington firmly in the forefront of commerce which was to culminate in the birth of passenger railways. Although the Bishops of Durham retained some control until the 19th century the Quaker influence which began in 1660 accelerated with some speed and drew attention away from the church although the market square has never ceased to be the shopping focus. The reason why so few ancient buildings remain, however, is due to a disastrous fire in 1585.

As it lay along the Great North Road many important visitors passed through Darlington including Margaret Tudor on her way to marry James IV of Scotland. It was this marriage which eventually led to the birth of Mary Queen of Scots and her son King James VI of Scotland becoming James 1st of England in 1603. He passed through Darlington on the death of Elizabeth to claim the inheritance from the Queen who had no heir of her own. She had to acknowledge the right of the son of her cousin Mary Queen of Scots who had been executed on Elizabeth's orders. This must have been a joyous occasion as the new King travelled south. Not so joyous was the passage northwards of the troops of the Duke of Cumberland harrying and butchering the Scot's army defeated in the 1745 rebellion which brought the Stuart line to such a sad end.

There can be no doubt that present day Darlington owes its proud recent history to the Quaker families, especially the Peases and the Backhouses. The Peases built efficient woollen mills along the banks of the Skerne. The Backhouses developed their own banks not geographical but financial. To instil confidence, piles of sovereigns were placed on the counters, thus preventing worried customers from withdrawing funds. The ploy certainly worked for business blossomed and eventually grew into Barclays Bank now one of the country's big 'high street' financial institutions.

Locally, however, the most important family was the Peases and it is quite right that the statue of Joseph Pease should dominate the part of the town near the Kings Head Hotel on the site of the coaching inn where so much important business was done. It was Edward Pease who promoted the construction of the Stockton to Darlington railway and had the foresight to employ Robert Stephenson from nearby Newcastle as the engineer. When the first steam driven system opened in 1825 the Quaker Railway as it became know focused the attention not only of Britain but of the world on the little textile town. Darlington for a while became the engineering centre of the world and it still retains some influence at the present time. The railway town developed rapidly and some of the original stretches of the Stockton and Darlington are still used today and British

North Road railway station at Darlington was built by the Stockton and Darlington railway company in 1842, is now a museum.

Rail's 'Heritage Line' linking Bishop Auckland, Darlington, Middlesbrough and Saltburn is well worth following. There are also summer Sunday trips to Stanhope in Upper Weardale. For the complete history however, a visit to the Railway Centre and Museum is a must. It is within walking distance of the Town Centre and opens all the year round between 9.30 am and 5 pm. It is situated at the North Road Passenger station built in 1842 to serve the Stockton to Darlington and which has been beautifully restored. The exterior looks like a cotton merchant's house in the southern states of America, its pale walls gleaming even in the merest shaft of sunlight. The entrance hall, ticket office and train shed have all been restored, not only as a museum of the Stockton and Darlington, but also of the North Eastern Railway Company. In 1991 a model railway showing the original route was opened, but it is the unique collection of engines which attract visitors from far and wide and also increasing numbers of educational trips. In the 1920s Darlington held regular railway carnivals and in 1991 this feature was revived and includes a colourful parade, craft fair, floats, steam rides and a fireworks display.

On permanent display are Stephenson's *Rocket* or rather a model of it, and, in our opinion, the much more impressive

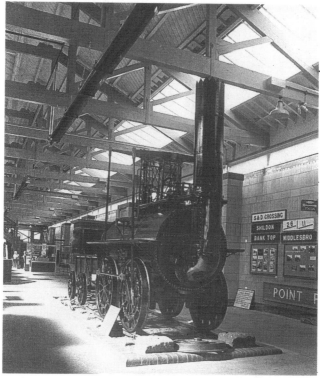

The Locomotion on display at the Darlington railway museum.

Locomotion Number One. The *Rocket* looks very small and was obviously a prototype whilst the *Locomotion* was obviously built to do a job over a long period of time. The engine shows all the evidence of the love which Stephenson bestowed upon it as he personally tightened every bolt and rivet. It looks like every boy's dream - a meccano model brought to life. Behind *Locomotion* on the wall of the station platform is a photograph taken in 1925 to commemorate the centenary of the opening and a very fine event it looks to have been. *Locomotion No. 1* looks as if it will be fit enough in 2025 to take part in the next celebration of the history of passenger railways. John Dobbin painted the original scene showing the first train

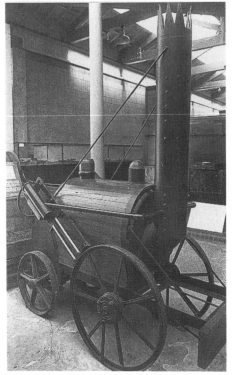

A model of Stephenson's Rocket is yet another historic exhibit on show at Darlington's railway museum.

passing over the bridge spanning the River Skerne, a proud structure which still stands today. Also on display is a railway carriage built in 1846 for the Stockton to Darlington and which looks just like a stagecoach lifted directly off the Turnpike roads of the period. It even has the upper section adapted with the space once used by driver and passengers functioning as a luggage area. The reason why the railway gauge of the world is standardised at 4 feet $8^{1}/_{2}$ inches is that this was the width of an old stage coach. Stephenson had enough trouble with engineering the track and the locomotives without having to redesign the wagons. The tradition of building locomotives only came to an end with

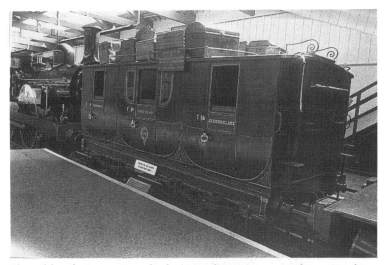

This old railway carriage looks just what it is — an adaptation from an old road stagecoach.

the closing of the British Rail workshops in 1966. This event was recorded in the *Northern Echo* the first halfpenny newspaper to be published in England back in 1869. The *Echo* is still going as is some heavy engineering and the Cleveland Bridge and Engineering Works has built many world famous spans including Australia's Sydney Harbour Bridge. Despite the coming of heavy metal, Darlington still retains more than a hint of the classical pastoral especially around the market place. It is possible to walk around the market hall - literally - as the Victorian arcaded structure huddles beneath the shadow of the town clock. This is a mixture of ancient and modern as the town hall was opened by HRH Princess Anne in the 1970s. On the forecourt is an interesting piece of metal sculpture by John Hoskins and which celebrates the recovery of the town after the closure of the railway works which coincided with the replacement of steam by diesel.

Apart from achieving world fame in the history of railways, Darlington also played its part in agriculture, particularly cattle breeding. Durham Shorthorns brought

In 1925 a re-run of the Stockton-to-Darlington passenger railway was organised to celebrate a century of the service. Here Locomotion is seen hard at work.

high prices and many of the town's fine Georgian houses were financed by the profits of beasts which were exported all over the world. The Quakers were also involved in this industry and they tended to live close together in an area of the town known as the West End. There is still a cattle market on Monday and Thursday, wool is spun and some engineering has survived.

From Darlington the Tees runs towards the sea and prior to the 1974 changes formed the boundary between County Durham and Yorkshire. Stockton was once in Durham and we have therefore included it in the present chapter. From Stockton the industrial Tees estuary is soon reached with Middlesbrough on the Yorkshire side and Hartlepool on the Durham bank. This once important town is described in chapter 8.

Stockton-on-Tees is the other end of the Stockton to Darlington railway and was once a market town vital to the surrounding district. It still is and is surrounded by a number of attractive small towns and villages. A visit to Stockton should begin with a long exploration of the Green Dragon museum situated in Theatre Yard. There is also an Information Centre here and provides an opportunity to keep up to date with attractions which seem to be sprouting in this area like mushrooms after a fall of September rain.

Stockton retains the traditional feel of a busy market town and its High Street is overlooked by its impressive Town Hall and market cross which are more than 250 years old. High Street is said to be the widest in Britain and it needs to be to hold the impressive market. On Wednesday and Friday an open market is held, continuing a trend began as long ago as 1310. Running off the High Street are fascinating alleys known as yards. Their names alone make them worth exploring and include Theatre Yard in which is situated the Green Dragon museum but there is also a Green Dragon yard itself, Hambletonian Yard and Wasp's Nest Yard. These are the places to discover grand old inns, a Georgian theatre and there are several points leading to the riverside. There is ample evidence here to show that Stockton was indeed on the Tees and was once an important port. The docks have now been largely landscaped to produce a pleasant and often breezy walkway. Some connection with the old port is maintained in late April or early May when the Stockton Regatta which has been held for more than 200 years takes place. This is the biggest tidal Regatta to be held in England. In November Stockton hosts a spectacular fireworks display.

Stockton developed from a market town to a major industrial settlement during the reign of Queen Victoria and mainly because of the Stockton and Darlington railway. The Old Ticket Office on Bridge Street has been converted into a small museum concerned with this historic line and complements the museum at Darlington.

Developments during this period swept away what was left of Stockton Castle which as usual was the property of the Bishops of Durham from medieval times. Modern developments have swamped or removed many of the Victorian buildings but High Street remains. So does the memory of two of Stockton's sons. John Walker invented the friction match, but forgot to take out a patent. We have got

Church Row at Stockton-on-Tees, photographed in 1902 and showing pigs on the way to market. The town has become much more industrialised these days.

so used to striking a match that we forget what life was like previously. People used tinder boxes which involved striking flints to create a spark. This caused cotton wool soaked in salt petre to catch fire. Before cotton people used to collect coltsfoot plants and pull off the seeds from the flowers and scrape the hairs off the leaves. Thomas Sheraton was born in 1751 at Stockton and learned the craft of furniture making here before moving to London to attract rich customers.

Although much of Stockton has gone the Green Dragon Yard Museum and Preston Hall Museum and Park have collected enough buildings and artefacts to tell an accurate story. Like Beamish, Preston Hall set in 117 acres (67 hectares) of park land, is fast becoming one of the major attractions in the North of England. It is situated on the A135 between Stockton and Yarm, and the hall was built by the shipbuilder and owner Sir Robert Ropner in 1825. There is a small parking fee but entry to the grounds and the house is free. There is an open air Victorian Street which was brought from

Stockton and working craftsmen are on site. On display are collections of costume, pewter and children's games. There is also an interesting collection of paintings with the most famous being the *Dice Players*. This is one of only three works in Britain by Georges de la Tour a 17th century French artist. Few town museums can compare with this one which has the added attraction of being free!

Beyond Preston Hall is Yarm, another market town which was also once an important port and lies in a loop of the River Tees. Its trade consisted of coal, lead and farm produce and ships worked their way up the Tees to avoid the dangerous mud flats. These were eventually dredged during the building of Middlesbrough on the Yorkshire bank of the Tees and the huge chemical complexes of Billingham on the old County Durham side. To us the fact that these now form part of Cleveland matters not! Yarm is still part of old County Durham. It is closer to the sea than Stockton and in the past high tides, wind and heavy rain have caused flooding. On the walls of the Town Hall, built in 1710 are marks showing the levels reached by the particularly bad floods of 1771 and 1881.

On the wall of the George and Dragon Hotel is a plaque which records the first meeting of the Stockton and Darlington Railway Company. A huge 43-arched viaduct built in 1851 appropriately dominates the town.

Yarm was given its charter by King John in 1207, who granted a weekly market and two annual fairs. A reminder of the latter is the three day October street fair which is still frequented by gypsies and showmen. At the peak of its prosperity, before it was upstaged by Middlesbrough, Yarm built ships and exported nails, rope, barrels, paper, clocks, leather and beer. The impressive Georgian houses at the southern end of High Street bear witness to the big profits which were made, and how some of them were spent.

Yarm has a couple of ancient architectural treasures, a church and a bridge. The church dedicated to St Mary Magdalene stands very much as it was rebuilt around 1730, but there had been very much older buildings on the same site. At the west end of the church are a few bits of the previous structure. There is a Friarage built in 1770 on the site of a Dominican friary, a remnant of this being an impressive Tudor dovecote. These were not merely decorative, but as pigeons breed all the year round a regular supply of young birds could be guaranteed to provide food in the days before refrigeration ensured a regular supply of meat. Running off the main street are a number of alleyways here called wynds and on Capel Wynd is an octagonal shaped Methodist chapel built in 1763 and much admired by John Wesley. We have seen an even earlier chapel at Heptonstall in West Yorkshire on which this design is obviously based and which Wesley is said to have helped to design.

Yarm bridge is said to have been constructed around 1400 on the orders of Prince Bishop Skirlaw and was an important crossing point of the Tees. In 1643 during the Civil War a skirmish was fought around the bridge and the dead were interred in the cemeteries of several local villages. The bridge once carried an important Turnpike road leading to the North and onwards to Scotland which accounts for the number of impressive old inns situated in the High Street and which still cater well for tourists.

Wandering around the town and along the riverside walk beyond the church and known as True Lovers Walk it is hard to imagine that you are close to one of the largest chemical complexes in the world. This is based around Billingham, and its Transporter Bridge opened in 1911 and connected Port Clarence to Middlesbrough and which still operates. At one time huge backlogs of traffic waited to be ferried across the 571 foot gap but thankfully these are now part of history since the opening of a bypass as part of the much improved A19. Passing Billingham at night is like a glimpse into Dante's Inferno - smoke, flame, steam and coloured light illuminating the sky and only the smell of petrochemicals spoils the illusion. Despite the presence of such heavy industry wildlife on the river has survived and on the mud flats around Seal Sands waders such as redshank, knot, dunlin and bar tailed godwits are to be seen on most days in the winter when populations are at their maximum.

Billingham did not begin to expand until 1834 when the railway arrived followed by glassworks and iron foundries.

This view of Yarm High street dates to around 1900. Apart from the presence of modern traffic many features remain unaltered.

During the First World War the seeds of the present chemical industry were sown as explosives and fertilisers were produced in an attempt to meet an ever increasing demand.

History tells us that there was a Saxon settlement here and the church of St Cuthbert has retained its Saxon tower and nave. This still overlooks the old village green even though this has now been surrounded by the town. Surprisingly all the ancient atmosphere has been retained especially during the Billingham International Folklore Festival which takes place each August. Billingham has a Monday market, the Forum complex includes an impressive ice rink, swimming pool and a theatre. The Art gallery is impressively varied and proves that Teesside is able to combine chemistry with culture.

Industry has also failed to completely swamp the ancient history of Thornaby-on-Tees which was at one time called South Stockton. Thornaby probably began as a Danish settlement around AD 800 and was mentioned in the Doomsday book. As with Billingham the ancient village green has survived and is overlooked by the church of St Peter ad Vincula which dates to the 11th century but with some excellent 12th century architecture. Very sensibly the centre has now been designated as a conservation area and includes a farmhouse with an 18th century rear and 19th front and Sundial house which bears a datestone reading 1621. Stockton Racecourse is also close by. From 1840 a railway link arrived and a bridge across the Tees enabling iron works, shipyards and bottle factories to develop at great speed and with little thought of planning. Until 1962 Thornaby was an important RAF base and this has now become the focus for new industries. The centre is now pedestrianised and there is a thriving Thursday market and the Pavilion is a leisure and indoor sports venue of the highest standard.

Lower Teesdale saw the birth of railways and the Stockton and Darlington has been the main thread running through this chapter. A more modern thread is tourism and the publicists working for this area have much to build upon. Industries which have gone should be integrated into discovery trails and the point made that modern industry and tourism are not necessarily counter-productive. This delicate balance is equally obvious around Bishop Auckland and Upper Weardale, the subject of the next chapter.

CHAPTER 4

Bishop Auckland and Upper Weardale

We know of several visitors to County Durham who have driven around Bishop Auckland having read travel writers who feel that the town is an untidy industrial sprawl. We feel sad that such travellers have been robbed of enjoying the magnificent town centre and the Palace which has been the home of the Prince Bishops of Durham for centuries.

The Bishop's Palace is the place to start after parking in the town square and passing through an arch surmounted by a clock. Auckland 'castle' opens between May and September on Tuesday mornings, Wednesday, Thursday and Sunday afternoons, Saturday afternoon in August and Bank Holiday Mondays. There is a small admission charge. As we have seen in other chapters of this book the Prince Bishops had the powers of Royalty and had a number of official and often fortified residences of which Auckland was the most important outside Durham itself. Several monarchs have been entertained here including John, Edward III, James I, Charles I and Victoria. Since Durham Castle was given to the University, Auckland has been the principal residence and official offices of the Bishop of Durham. The Castle is set on a prominent hill above the River Wear and its tributary the Gaunless. Both the castle and the one time deer park which surrounds it have been part of the Prince Bishop's estate since the 12th century. The park land of around 800 acres (320 hectares) is open daily free of charge and a nature trail has been laid out and which is so rich in natural history that a whole day could be spent following it. Those who love walking should also sample the Bishop Brandon Walk which runs $9^1/2$ miles from Bishop Auckland to the Broompark Picnic Site which is on the edge of the city of Durham. This crosses the now disused railway viaduct from which there are wonderful views over the Wear Valley. Our list of birds spotted in the park and along the Bishop Brandon Walk during the late April day of sunshine and showers included woodcock, common sandpiper, jay, great spotted woodpecker, nuthatch, spotted flycatcher, and chiff chaff.

Apart from the rich natural history available for free it is also worth the entry fee to enjoy the history of the castle. The jewel in the Prince Bishop's architectural crown is St Peter's, said to be the largest private chapel in Europe. It was built in the 12th century by Hugh le Puiset not originally as a chapel but as a sumptuous banqueting hall. It continued in this function until after the period of Oliver Cromwell's Commonwealth following which Bishop John Cosin spent lavishly but wisely on converting the building into a chapel. There were already fine columns and arches with buttresses added in the 13th century by Bishop Beck plus some highly decorative woodwork but Cosin added his own imaginative touches. In the north east are a set of six windows telling the history of Christianity and other glass given by Bishop Lightfoot in the 19th century adds glorious colour to this delightful building.

The Throne room is also something special with the main feature being the ornate throne set against a plaster screen depicting the arms of the Diocese in general and those of Bishop Barnofton in particular and who was here in the late 18th century. The walls are covered with portraits of past bishops. The Wyatt ceiling is also impressive but it is a pity that it is false and beneath it is a medieval raftered ceiling.

The long dining room is an early 16th century structure commissioned by Cuthbert Tunstall who was the last Catholic bishop prior to Henry VIII's confrontation with the Pope and the subsequent Reformation. The ceiling is magnificent as are the life sized portraits of Jacob and his twelve sons, the work of the Spaniard Francesco Zurburan. This and the old Banqueting Hall prove that the Bishops dined in wonderful surroundings.

The bright market square has been in use since medieval times, no doubt developing mainly to serve the needs of the castle. Since a one way system has funnelled the through traffic away from the centre a more relaxed, almost continental atmosphere has developed. Even the inroads made by industry have failed to obliterate the little villages which were once close to Bishop Auckland and St Andrew

The entrance to the Bishop's Park at Bishop Aukland.

Auckland, South Church, St Helen Auckland and especially
West Auckland are all attractive. The village green running
the length of the latter village is its most beautiful feature.

Bishop Auckland has its own history concerned with
medieval England, but close by are even older settlements.
At Binchester there is a glimpse of Imperial Rome whilst
Saxon England is seen in all its glory at Escomb. Binchester
Roman Fort is signed from the centre of Bishop Auckland

The Bishop's official residence at Bishop Aukland viewed through its impressive gateway.

near the town hall which itself is a Grade 1 listed building and which during 1992 underwent an expensive restoration programme in preparation for a 1993 opening. It now houses library, arts exhibitions and Tourist Information Centre. The road from it runs alongside the River Wear beside which are plenty of parking places. From these are splendid views of the Bishop's Palace and the railway viaduct. The late summer riverside vegetation includes lots of thistles, willowherb and knapweed all of which attracts a host of butterflies such as peacock, meadow brown, small tortoiseshell and orange tip. The Roman fort is situated just behind Binchester Hall, a Georgian building now used as a nursing home. The Romans knew the fort as Vinovia and the fort was one of a chain of such structures which protected the road (Dere Street) running from York to Hadrian's wall. It was built about AD80 and such was its permanence and importance that additions and alterations were being made throughout the occupation which lasted until the end of the fourth century AD. Even after the Romans left there is plenty of evidence to show that the Saxons used the fort. This occupied around 10 acres (4 hectares) and students of the period have calculated that it would have supported 500 cavalry plus other troops and all the necessary support services.

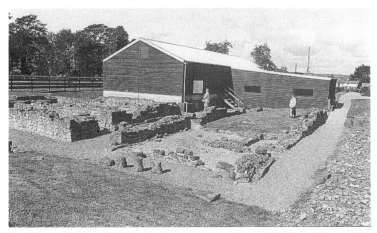

The Roman fort at Binchester deserves greater credit than it has so far been given.

The commander of such an impressive fort must have lived in great luxury, but much of the evidence of this lies buried beneath the surrounding fields. What does survive and is in the process of being excavated is the commander's bath house, the most complete such structure to be seen in England. It is administered by the Bowes Museum for the Durham County council Binchester Bath House is open between April and September each day except Thursday and Friday. It opens at 10.30 am and closes at 6 pm. The bath house was built in the early part of the 4th century and its design would still be attractive to the patrons of a modern day health club. The bather first entered a changing room and then slipped on a pair of wooden sandals to protect the feet from the heated duct under the floor. The first three rooms were all warm but got hotter as the bather moved through. The third room was heated by a charcoal furnace and recent experiments have shown that the tiles and floor concrete held the heat in just the same manner as a modern storage heater. The Romans were skilful producers of cement and produced a pinkish colour by adding crushed tiles to the mixture. The idea of all these hot rooms was to produce a sweat in much the same way as a sauna. The bather was

The excavated bath house at the Roman fort of Binchester. This is the most complete bath house of its period to be found in Britain.

provided with scrapers with which to remove any grease and grime. After this the bather plunged first into hot water which sounds good to us and then into a cold plunge which we could do without!

There are plans for further excavations at Binchester and also to generate more publicity. All this is absolutely essential because Binchester should be regarded as a major Roman site and we feel that in time a major museum on the lines of those along Hadrian's Wall must surely develop.

Although the Saxons made some use of Binchester the real gem of their period is at Escomb. Here is the least disturbed Saxon church to be found in the whole of England. Nobody knows for sure when the church was built or who built it, but archaeologists are able to make some accurate assumptions from its fabric. The church is always kept locked but the three keys needed to gain entry can be obtained from 22 Saxon Green, a house opposite the church. The keys are hung on the door of the house between 9 am and 8 pm in summer and until 4 pm in winter. Inside there is lots of explanatory literature but guided tours can be arranged by contacting the vicar.

Escomb village, its greens, post office, toilets, houses ancient and modern, and the Saxon Inn are set around the circular churchyard. This is surrounded by a stone wall with the circular shape indicating its Celtic origin. There is a local tradition that the church may be on the site of a Roman temple but the stones incorporated into the church could have come from Binchester. Roman and Saxon coins have been found on the site and the presence of a Roman settlement should not be discounted. Some of these coins and other artefacts are on display in the porch.

The church itself is attractive on the outside, but the interior is truly awe-inspiring in its height and even its plainness has atmosphere. Apart from historians, naturalists also plan regular visits to Escomb. This is because of the presence of a colony of whiskered bats which enter the church via gaps in the stone roof and they roost in the roof boards on which they hang by their feet upside down. Bats do no damage and their droppings lack both water and dangerous bacteria. Since the late 1980s bats have been protected by law and groups now regularly inspect roosts and count populations. The whiskered bat (Myotis myntacinus) is by no means common especially in the North of England. They have their own hunting beat which they patrol throughout the night and, in spring and autumn, when food must be gathered, they may be seen hunting by day usually up to 72 feet (20 metres) above ground level. In

The Saxon church at Escomb is one of the best preserved in Europe.

appearance, the whiskered bat lives up to its name, having hairs around its lips forming a moustache as well as other groups of bristles along the forehead and chin. The female is slightly larger than the male and the head and body usually measure less than 2 inches (5 centimetres) although the wing span is more than double this.

On sale in the church and at the nearby Saxon Inn are a couple of leaflets describing local walks, one described as the Bishop's Path and the other as a Time Walk. The walk follows the bank of the Wear and in the summer we have watched the common sandpiper bobbing up and down on the pebbles of the riverside whilst goosanders can be seen throughout the year but are much more common in the winter. The Time Walk leads through the remnants of the old iron mining industry but parts follow an ancient route used by Celts, Romans and Saxons. At one time the course of the Wear was much closer to the village which stood upon a vital crossing point.

It is, however, the ecclesiastical history of Escomb which is of national importance and the church should be explored

The sundial over the porch at Escomb.

at leisure. Although the first written evidence relating to what was then called 'Edicum' was during the 10th century when the Saxon bishop of Durham mortgaged the area to a group of Viking Earls, although the deed was later redeemed. This proves that a building actually existed and archaeologists have dated the church to between 670 and 690. One further deduction was made by the experts and that is the height of the narrow church suggests Irish origins. Here then we have one of the North East's most ancient churches along with Monkwearmouth and Jarrow described elsewhere in this book and the building on Holy Island described in our companion volume *Discovering Northumberland*.

Immediately on entering the church one is struck by the chancel arch which is probably a re-assembled Roman archway which either existed on site or was perhaps brought from Binchester. In the north wall there is a stone inscribed with Roman lettering now set into the Saxon window sill and some stones with diamond shaped broaching are also Roman in origin. Beneath the arch, faded scroll work paintings which have caused some disagreement among experts, some feeling that they are 12th or 13th century but others feel that they could be contemporary with the building of the church. On the wall opposite the entrance is a very faded wall painting which is part of an ancient Saint and it is thought that in its prime the church may have been decorated with portraits of as many as four Saints. The octagonal font which is still used for baptisms may also be Saxon, but is more likely to be of the 10th or early 11th century. Its shape suggests that infants in those far off days were fully immersed in the holy water and there is also evidence that the font was once covered and locked. This was necessary during the dark days when those engaged in the occult made use of holy water in their evil practices.

The barn-like cross beams of the high roof may well be Saxon, but other woodwork in this area dates to the period of restoration between 1875 and 1880. In the 1960s oak pews and electric lighting were added, but these do nothing to detract from the ancient feel of this building and are in any case very necessary for the comforts of the Sunday morning communicants.

It is not just the interior of Escomb which is of interest as there are Saxon crosses, very old sundials and some of the earliest examples of gravestones.

In the porch there are the remnants of two stone crosses close to the display cases containing the Roman coins already mentioned. One cross is inscribed with a bird and a vine and the other is so simple that experts feel that it may never have been finished. The little bits of Saxon glass which may have been made around Jarrow and the crosses may well be late 7th century in origin.

Escomb has two fascinating sundials. On the south wall is a dial dating to the 7th century and is thought to be the earliest such structure still in its original position to be found in Britain. Its design shows an animal above a serpent which shows a similarity to a Teutonic pagan god brought to the north country by the invading Saxons. It may be that this is an early Christian attempt to absorb pagan gods and the scratch marks on the dial probably indicate the times of services. The sundial above the porch is a more traditional type.

The skull and crossbones on a gravestone shown here at Escomb did not have the modern piratical meaning way back in medieval times. It was simply a sign of death.

Close to the entrance of the church are two intriguing gravestones of medieval origin. One bears a cross, one has a cross and a pair of shears and both are thought to have been a memorial to a local knight and his lady. The skull and cross bones in those days did not have the piratical overtones of more recent times, but merely registering a hope of the afterlife.

Visitors often wonder why Escomb church should have retained all its Saxon features through the Victorian period when the urge to restore was almost synonymous with legalised vandalism. The Saxon building was so run down that a brand new church was built at the top of the village. Later the Saxon building was accurately restored and the later church has since been demolished. Its position is marked only by a graveyard.

There was also a Saxon church at Brancepeth and the first written records relate to the appointment of a rector in 1085. At that time the parish stretched from Lanchester to Croxdale and from the borders of Durham City to Wolsingham. The Rector of Brancepeth still appoints the vicars of Brandon, Crook, Waterhouses and Willington.

We arrived at Brancepeth on a warm Sunday in late August and were immediately struck by the smell of roses, the sight of ripe blackberries, rosehips and rowan and the tangle of cottages overlooked by the bulk of the castle. Beyond the church and fringed by trees is the church of St Brandon. Brandon was an Irish Saint which suggests that here was possibly a 6th century religious centre.

The castle's origins are probably Saxon and was important in the affairs of the county especially when it passed by marriage into the hands of the Neville family during the 13th century. Following the Rising of the North in 1569, Brancepeth and its lands became forfeit and it was never again a focal point in affairs beyond the village. In 1796 William Russell, who made a substantial fortune from his coal mines, refurbished church and castle. In the 1830s his son Matthew employed the architect John Patterson to produce an unusual castle. Here are huge towers which look like chess pieces, great solid curtain walls and an imposing entrance blocked by a portcullis. At one time the castle was the headquarters of the Durham Light Infantry but it is now a private house. There is no doubt that it would make a splendid museum but the church is so delightful that a steady stream of visitors is ensured. St Brandon's was described by Pevsner who wrote that 'There is hardly another church in the country so completely and splendidly furnished'.

Brancepeth Castle — a fascinating mix of ancient and modern with its towers modelled on chess pieces.

The tower is 12th century, part of the nave built in the 13th and extended in the 14th century and at this time transepts were added and the aisles widened. The roof of the aisle has its original 14th century roof. As with all famous Churches the furnishings of St Barndon's are impressive and cover several centuries. In the chancel is a larger-than-life stone effigy of the "Peacock of the North'. This was the nickname given to Robert Neville who during the 14th century lived a tempestuous life and seemed intent upon fighting at every opportunity. It is therefore not surprising that he is shown in full armour and his head surrounded by a bevy of priests praying for the soul of this tempestuous knight. In the north transept are wooden effigies which can be read like a history text. They are of the Second Earl of Westmoreland and his wife and on their collars they wear the white rose of York. At one time a white bear was hanging from the Duke's collar but this has been lost. This was the symbol of Richard III who spent much of his short and tragic reign in the North of England, especially around Richmond. He married Anne Neville. The Earls of Westmoreland also belonged to the Neville family and the effigy of the Earl has his head resting on a boar. This was part of the family crest of the Nevilles who took it from the Bulmers who were at

Brancepeth church — one of the finest in County Durham, and set in delightful surroundings.

Brancepeth before the Conquest. The two were joined by a marriage of a male Neville with a Bulmer heiress.

On the north wall is another history lesson in the form of a wooden plaque. This was put up by John Cosin who became the Bishop of Durham at the time of the Restoration of Charles II. Cosin had been rector at Brancepeth in 1625 and so in his old living he commemorated his own life along with a celebration of the return of the monarchy after years of high church suppression by the Cromwellian Common-wealth. Cosin provided the church with a great deal of its furnishings including the chancel woodwork. The reredos are even earlier being provided by Prior Castell during the 15th century.

On entering the church four unusual artefacts can be seen. Just inside the door is a small black helmet which looks to be of iron but is in fact made of wood painted black. This was once carried to funerals on the coffin of local dignitaries. Facing the door is the font which should be examined closely. It is made of Frosterley marble and a close look at its smoothed surface will reveal large numbers of fossils. The quarries around the village of Frosterley will be described later in this chapter. Beyond the font are two

This font of Frosterley marble is in Brancepeth church. The fossils in the stone can be clearly seen.

objects, one ancient and functional, the other modern and artistic but both fascinating. These are a medieval clock mechanism and a memorial to St Brandon. The latter shows a great deal of artistic licence but a great deal of skill in working the bits and pieces of iron painted black. It depicts the journey of St Brandon from Ireland to Britain. He would have travelled in a simple boat, perhaps made of leather but in any event his transport would not have been in an Elizabethan galleon. There is, however, a very impressive feel about the work, as there is about the whole of

Brancepeth village which has remained unspoiled and untouched by the 20th century.

The same cannot be said for Spennymoor which is very much a product of the industrial age but it is still an attractive place which is well worth discovering. Spennymoor is a Victorian town with modern tower blocks reflecting its function as a focal point for the mines which developed in the surrounding countryside but there are impressively attractive areas nearby including Whitworth Hall at Croxdale, Sedgefield, Newton Aycliffe, Shildon and Crook.

Whitworth Hall, set among almost 100 acres (40 hectares) of parkland, and deer have been emparked here since 1420 when permission was obtained to keep them. The Hall and Gardens open at weekends from Easter to the end of September and from Spring Bank Holiday onwards. Whitworth also opens on Monday, Tuesday and Wednesday from 11 am to 6 pm with the house closing at 5 pm and there is an entry fee. There is a pleasant tea room catering for visitors who mostly come to see the birthplace of the famous 'Bonnie Bobbie Shafto'. They also visit his grave in Whitworth churchyard. Whitworth Hall was purchased by the Shafto family in 1652 for the sum of £247 10s 0d. The house is in excellent condition and visitors can see the library, kitchen and laundry on the ground floor whilst upstairs is a modern day connection with the fiery Bishop Jenkins, formerly of Durham. His wife Molly and her friends have made a model village with a mansion, fun fair and market all accurately and painstakingly fashioned.

Great restoration work has been done in the gardens and grounds with two original lakes having been re-dug. There is plenty of space for visitors to picnic and dogs are welcome but should be kept on a lead. Plans are well advanced to provide small steam trains and launches on the lakes all proving that Bonnie Bobby Shafto lived in a very Bonny spot.

Croxdale is situated on the old Great North Road although facing it these days are miners cottages, but there is a bridge over the Wear which dates to the 13th century and below its more modern counterpart. Close by is a railway viaduct which carries the London to Edinburgh trains across the Wear. The district was controlled for many years by the

Salvin family. They came in the early 15th century but Croxdale Hall was rebuilt in the 18th century and it is not open to the public and alas almost hidden by magnificent trees. Burn Hall also belonged to the Salvins and dates to the 19th century and is now a Roman Catholic seminary.

Sedgefield has remained unspoiled despite being close to the industrial sprawl of Teesside and used as a dormitory by the workers. It remains a grand old market town with its famous racecourse, now separated from it by the A689 which runs from Billingham to Bishop Auckland.

The town centre is dominated by St Edmund's church built in the 13th century, and with the tower visible from many miles away. The name Sedgefield refers to the original dampness of the area before the church and the town was built. Bishop Cutheard founded the church around AD900 with the first structure being of wood, but soon after the Normans came a stone building replaced it. In AD1085 Ulchild was the first recorded rector, who was also designated the Lord of the Manor. This meant that the post was both lucrative and influential. Between 1246 and 1256 the present church was built and dedicated to St Edmund associated with the Bishop and Edmund Rich the Archbishop of Canterbury. William the Conqueror ordered that a curfew bell was to be rung each evening at 9 pm and the great pity is that the custom was discontinued in 1965. We are always sad when such connections with Old England are severed. One custom which has been retained is the Shrove Tuesday football match although the description may well infringe the Trades Descriptions Act. A ball is passed through the bull ring on the green at 1 pm and then thrown into the crowd. The whole town is used as the pitch with the two teams drawn from the farmers on one side and the traders on the other.

The view of this event from the church tower is remarkable, the huge solid structure being built in the 15th century at the expense of a local man named Robert Rhodes. The clock in the tower is not the original but bought to celebrate Queen Victoria's Jubilee in 1897. The tower was restored in the late 1980s and inside the church are some interesting furnishings.

The church of St Edmund at Sedgefield.

Just after entering the church by the south door, look at the north door which is kept shut. In the superstitious days of medieval times this door was kept open and was supposed to let the devil out before the service began. It was then bolted to keep him out. A similar north door can be seen in other churches including Escomb.

The chancel screen should not be missed as it is another connection with Bishop Cosin of Durham whose influence spread throughout the county. The screen is a fine example of Elizabethan woodworking, more of which can be seen in

Durham cathedral. It is probably the work of Robert Barker who was active in the 1630s and also did some carving at Brancepeth. Cosin's other connection with Sedgefield was through his son-in-law Denis Grenville who was rector of Sedgefield between 1567 and 1690. This is fact but the story of the Pickled Parson is the stuff of folklore and fiction rather than fact.

Just at the time that the tithes were due to be paid to the rector he fell ill and died. His wife realised that she was not entitled to the tithes and the following year was likely to be hard for her. She therefore pickled the body in salt and kept it hidden until the day the tithes were due. When the villagers of Sedgefield arrived to pay they saw the rector propped up in his chair but too ill to speak. On the following day the lady announced that her husband was dead. We guess that there have been many rectors who enjoyed a glass or two, but none was quite so under the influence as this Pickled Parson.

From the church we strolled around the town square which has retained its old pump and also the atmosphere within its numerous old inns which once served travellers along the old coaching routes of the late 18th and early 19th centuries. Feelings of the equestrian days return on race days, when the colours of the flowers which seem to burst from the cottages and hanging baskets blend with the outfits of those enjoying the sport of Kings. Fox hunting is also popular hereabouts with the kennels of the South Durham Hunt situated close to the town. There is also an important agricultural show which takes over the town every August, details of which are published well in advance. Like all of County Durham Sedgefield is within range of excellent walking with Hardwick Hall Country Park close by.

Newton Aycliffe is an intriguing mixture of ancient Aycliffe with the first of County Durham's new-towns built around it beginning in 1947. Aycliffe's church has Saxon origins but mostly dates to the 12th century and is quickly reached from the A167 which lies on the route of the old Great North Road. This lies on the south side of the road whilst away to the east is the comparatively busy A1(M). The town planners here have had most of their initial aims

The old pump in the centre of Sedgefield, a most attractive market town.

realised as the Newton part of the Aycliffe still has a village atmosphere about it despite the industrial and housing estates which have been built since its inception. The approach to the complex is still through fields, wooded copses and rich hedgerows full of summer flowers and autumn berries.

Shildon on the other hand, looks just what it is - a working town, but one with a rich heritage well told in the Timothy Hackworth Victorian Railway Museum. It is well signed from the town centre and opens from Easter Friday to the last Sunday in October daily except Monday and Tuesday from 10 am to 5 pm and at other times by appointment. This is one of the most important railway museums in the world. Timothy Hackworth was a pioneer of locomotive powered railways and in his own way deserves equal credit with the Stephensons. The son of a blacksmith Timothy became the superintendent engineer for the Stockton and Darlington railway from 1825 to 1840. Two years after this enterprise opened the steam powered locomotives proved so unreliable that the company reluctantly decided to return to horses. Hackworth was not at all pleased and decided to build his own locomotive. In 1827 his *Royal George* engine was produced, proved totally reliable and the future of steam powered railways was ensured, at a time when investors were proving to be very reluctant. Timothy Hackworth was also a pioneer in the export of locomotives which he built at Shildon. An engine went to Canada in 1836 another to Russia in 1837 and his last locomotive was the *Sans Pareil No 2* which reached a speed of more than 80 mph in 1849. Hackworth's *Sans Pareil No 1* was entered for the Rainhill trials but on the day was beaten by Stephenson's *Rocket*. It could not have been envisaged that Hackworth's locomotives were more reliable, an engineering proof of the moral of the tortoise and the hare. The literature on sale at the museum boasts that Timothy Hackworth was the greatest locomotive engineer that ever lived - after visiting his old workshops and after a great deal of critical reading we find it hard to argue with this boast.

The museum is based at Soho Cottage, which was the home of Timothy and his family from 1831. This has been restored to reflect the social conditions of the time and family letters are on display and help to create the right atmosphere. The nearby Engine Shed houses a full scale replica of the *Sans Pareil* and this is kept in steam throughout the year. The shed itself is also remarkable for its unique heating system. Adding to the atmosphere is the world's oldest Coal Manager's office and even stables which Timothy was largely instrumental in replacing are also part of the museum complex. Although now apparently isolated behind a housing estate the Hackforth buildings were once at the centre of a network of railway tracks, initially horse drawn, which connected the local coal mines to their distributors. Some of these routes are now followed by a series of Railway Walks which are described on display boards and on leaflets on sale in the museum. One of the trails leads to Shildon terminus and another stretch to the Brusselton incline both of which were stretches on the original Stockton and Darlington railway along which passengers were first conveyed in converted coal wagons. It was a sad day when in 1985 British Rail finally closed the last line to the wagon works.

Crook derives its name from an obvious bend in the River Wear and after a period of being dominated by coal mining the town is now cleaner and is the administrative centre of this district of Weardale. The town centre is now an open area which in summer is a jumble of flowers, and to the north of the town is Billy Row which is a typical miners' settlement and a reminder of the town's industrial past.

Near Crook is the interesting village of Tow Law which earned its living not from coal but because of the Weardale Iron Foundry and their foundry is still in evidence in the town. Just as Middleton-in-Teesdale was a product of the London Lead Company so Tow Law was once owned by the Weardale Iron Company. Coal mines were also present in the area but both the iron and the coal are now worked out and what was once a working town is slowly becoming an agricultural village. There are cattle and sheep markets the local speciality being 'mule gimmer' which are cross-bred ewes and these are auctioned and despatched to all parts of Britain. The countryside theme is continued within the church where the one time vicar Thomas Espin (1888-1934) has decorated a screen in a most unusual manner. He carved acorns, walnuts, fir cones and chestnuts. The vicar did not only look down at the fruits of the earth but upwards towards the heavens and had an observatory built in the rectory garden.

Crook and Bishop Auckland are both ideal bases from which to reach the A689 which runs through Upper Weardale with stops made at Wolsingham, Hamsterley Forest, Frosterley, Stanhope, Eastgate, Westgate, Ireshopeburn, Cowshill and the Killhope Wheel Mining Centre.

A number of these Wearside villages including Wolsinghan and Stanhope are described in well presented and inexpensive town trails which provide even more evidence of the shift in emphasis from industry to tourism. Wolsingham still has the scars of industry, but its rural setting and recent developments have created something of a holiday atmosphere strengthened by the closeness of Tunstall reservoir and Hamsterley Forest. Both the River Wear and the reservoir are popular with anglers with sea and brown trout present and permits locally available. Tunstall provides good sport for bird watchers especially in winter and our January list included tufted duck, pochard, wigeon, goosander and Canada goose. In contrast Hamsterley is a forest for all seasons but visitors should be aware that there is a parking fee before access can be gained to the picnic site and Information Centre. This is County Durham's largest man made forest and occupies about 6500 acres (2500 hectares) and which was planted from 1927 following the purchase of the Surtees estate. The forest is large and varied enough to support badger, fox and red squirrel whilst the birds seen include wood warbler, goldcrest, crossbill, pied flycatcher and nuthatch. Not all the forest is dense and dark coniferous, but there are areas of deciduous wood with open canopy through which sunlight can penetrate and allow wild flowers such as primrose, bluebell, dog violet, foxglove and ladies mantle to thrive.

Bedburn Beck drains the whole of the forest and many of its tributary streams are fast flowing and provide damp habitats for an assortment of mosses, liverworts and some rare ferns including moonwort and adder's tongue. Flowering plants include opposite-leaved golden saxifrage, wood sorrel and ransoms. Grey wagtail and dipper both breed by the streams. In the drier patches we have found enough wild raspberries in June and early July to mix with cream and provide a sweet conclusion to our picnics. Rightly famous is the Pennington Beech wood which at 985 feet (300 metres) above sea level is one of the highest such woods in Britain and other native species present include alder, ash, willow and birch. At the Information Centre there is a detailed display concerned with the forest and at numerous points around the forest are car parks with ice cream carts and small mobile snack bars. The parking areas are so extensive that there always seems to be plenty of space and the marked walks are seldom too busy to prevent good watching.

Frosterley is on the A689 almost directly between the Wolsingham and Stanhope and the village is famous for its marble quarries. Its name originally meant the forest-lea. There are many old quarries in the area although all are now closed. The marble was famous throughout the country and beyond; at Brancepeth the font is an example of a polished block and there is another in Frosterley church which was only built in 1869. The font, however, is older and was brought from Gainsborough in Lincolnshire. The stone was also popular as a facing for expensive public buildings. An unpolished block is on display in Frosterley car park and the fossils from which it is formed can be clearly seen. Marble was formed as limestone was subjected to heat and pressure as the earth's crust moved and as conditions cooled causing it to recrystallise. This process is known to geologists as thermal metamorphism. Some 325 million years ago in a period known as the Carboniferous this area was covered by a warm shallow sea. In this clear sea many marine animals thrived including a type of coral named Dibuniphyllum. As generation after generation of this coral died it became buried and then crushed until layers of what we know today as Frosterley marble was formed. The Normans were the first to appreciate its properties and it was mentioned in the Boldon Book of 1183 commissioned by Prince Bishop Hugh de Puiset. He notes that the valuable deposits were in great demand and mention is made of 'Lambert the marble cutter.' Frosterley marble was used in the construction of the Chapel of the Nine Altars and other parts of Durham Cathedral. The material was also used at the Bishop's Palace at Auckland Castle and much later in the foundation stone at Crook Council offices and at the Civic Centre small items made from Frosterley marble are on sale.

Although Frosterley village is little more that a line of ex-quarrymen's cottages it has its attractions and the old stone bridge on the outskirts of the town once carried the main road out of the village to Teesdale. This is now the B6278 and is well worth following as it passes a number of old quarries many of which are now car parks. They are popular pull-ins and in summer ice-cream and hot-dog stands do a roaring trade with sun-seekers and walkers. It is still our favourite route between Weardale and Teesdale but the purpose of this chapter is to follow the Wear up to Killhope. The next settlement up-dale is Stanhope.

Botanists flock to Stanhope, not to seek the blooms on the local moors or in woodlands, but because of the fossil tree now almost embedded into the churchyard wall. This was

Stanhope church.

found between Stanhope and Edmundbyers and has been identified as a giant plant similar to the small marestails which still grow today in the damp areas of the district. Some 250 million years ago what is now the moorlands of Upper Teesdale was a huge area of swampland full of giant trees. This one has been so long in the ground that it looks and feels as smooth as gun metal.

The church itself, dedicated to St Thomas, dates back to Norman times, but inside is a Roman altar proving that this area has been settled for much longer. The altar is dedicated to Silvanus the god of woodland. Artefacts from the Stone and Bronze Ages have been found in the area especially around Heatheryburn Cave which was discovered in 1843. Here was discovered the earliest form of wheeled transport ever found in Britain.

After the Romans came the Anglo Saxons who were both fierce and pagan. Christianity as we have indicated in the description of Escomb reached these parts from Ireland. Initially their worshipping had to be in secret and Linkirk Cave on the banks of the Shitlehopeburn, a tributary to the

The famous fossil tree in front of the church at Stanhope.

Wear, to the east of the town is one of these hidden meeting houses. Lin means a stream and kirk has obviously a religious origin. Stanhope is named from the same language with 'stan' meaning stoney and 'hope' meaning a valley.

Eventually the Saxon Christians felt confident enough to leave their secret cave and probably established a religious house on the present site, but it was the Normans who built the first stone structure. A Saxon font found in the church-yard has been moved into the church. The list of rectors runs from 1200 right up to the present day.

Initially Weardale provided the Prince Bishops with vast hunting grounds and in the 14th century the local bowmen were famous. Fifteen hundred were gathered on the orders of the Bishop to do battle with the Scots at Bannockburn. Very few returned. It was not long before the bowmen were replaced by lead men as the mineral deposits around Stanhope helped to swell the coffers of Bishops and provide work for an increasing population. Some of the profits were spent on the church. Inside there are some good examples of Frosterley marble furniture. The Bishops gave permission for a Friday market and three annual fairs one of which remains and is the popular Stanhope Show. Early markets were usually held in the churchyard and a cross was put up in 1699 only to be replaced almost 200 years later by the present cross just outside the church gates. The original cross can still be seen on the right hand side of the path leading up to the church. In the churchyard are a number of interesting tombs and gravestones including a coffin of Frosterley marble which probably dates to the Crusades.

Two rectors of the church at Stanhope achieved great distinction and became Bishops of Durham. Cuthbert Tunstall led an eventful life throughout the turbulent times of the Tudors. He began his ministry during the reign of Henry VIII. In the reign of Edward VI he was deprived of the rich living of Tunstall but Mary Tudor restored them thus indicating his preference for the Catholic faith. This was underlined by the fact that he refused to take the Oath of Supremacy demanded by Elizabeth 1st and was deprived again of his Stanhope living. At this time, however, he was old and ill and died within a couple of months. Apart from enjoying the money from his Stanhope Rectorship Tunstall had served as Bishop of London and then Durham both of which provided him with substantial financial rewards.

Joseph Butler (1692-1752) was rector at Stanhope and also went on to higher posts being appointed as bishop first of Bristol and then Durham. He earned a reputation as a learned theologian and his book *An Analogy of Religion* was famous in its time and is still read by theologians. Part of St Thomas's is devoted to a display of portraits of its past rectors which combined with other furnishings already described and some impressive wood carving both ancient and modern demand that time is taken to explore this church with care.

Two other buildings demand attention, Stanhope Castle and Stanhope Old Hall. Stanhope Castle occupies one corner of the square opposite the church and from this angle does not look at all impressive. Viewed from the river, however, it looks quite magnificent. The term castle is, however, misleading since it was built for Cuthbert Rippon the MP for Gateshead in 1798. It is a typical gentleman's residence of the period but was built on the site of an ancient castle and was used for a time as a school prior to being converted into flats.

To reach Stanhope Old Hall from the village the Durham Dales Centre with its modern Information Centre and toilets are passed on the right. The centre is open every day throughout the year and its aim is to provide a focus for developments in the area. Training courses, business advice and small business units are provided. There is a tea room decorated with murals which illustrate the history of Weardale and which are the work of students. One of these gives a picture of what conditions would have been like when the fossil tree was but a sapling. There is a shop and plenty of parking among well kept gardens. The Old Hall was built in the 17th century and is very impressive although some guide books suggest that it looks like a mill, but this is because some of the windows were blocked in to prevent the payment of window tax. We complain these days at community charges or rates, but this 19th century piece of effrontery was the first and last attempt to tax daylight! Nearby is Unthank Hall an even older house dating to Elizabethan times, the home of the Maddison family for many generations and like the Old Hall not open to the public but easily seen from the road without being intrusive. The word Unthank is of interest and means 'without leave'. This suggests that its origins may relate to squatters, but this did not have the same meaning as at present. There was a law which allowed any person to select a plot of land and provided they constructed a house with a roof from which smoke issued within 24 hours they were allowed to stay.

For the physically fit it is possible to walk from Stanhope almost the whole of the 25 miles to the City of Durham by following the Waskerley and Lanchester Valley Walkways which have been developed from redundant railways. The Stanhope and Tyne railway was an early development built to export lead, iron and limestone to the steel works of Consett and the rich farmlands of England and even abroad needed lime for the soil.

The next large settlement up Weardale after passing through Eastgate and Westgate, which mark the limits of the park where the Prince Bishops once hunted deer, is St John's Chapel. This is another village whose prosperity was once based firmly on the mining and quarrying industry. It is said to be the only village in County Durham which has a town hall! Like Frosterley the hillsides around St Johns are pockmarked with workings and these stony places provide nesting habitats for the summer visiting wheatears and the resident kestrels which are usually to be seen soaring about on the slightest of breezes and earning their local name of 'windhover'.

These days the lead miners have gone but the Upper Dale has not forgotten its social history and there are two excellent museums which should be visited. They should be regarded as complementary rather than competitors.

The Weardale Museum at Ireshopeburn was established in 1985 by a group of local enthusiasts. Amateurs they may be but this little museum is a professional set up without argument. It is situated in the old manse of the adjoining High House chapel which was built in 1760. Like many mining and quarrying communities the local folk were much influenced by John Wesley who often preached hereabouts between 1752 and 1788. His work in the area is described in the Wesley Room and the chapel in which he preached is still in use and can be opened on request. Other rooms include a Weardale kitchen of the 1890s, Railways of Weardale, Landscape and Wildlife and Water and Industry. The latter explains how the Burnhope reservoir was constructed flooding the village of Burnhope in the process. This was completed in the 1930s, and so there is a comprehensive photographic record of the process. The construction of water wheels to drive machinery and also to crush ore is explained and this links naturally with a visit to Killhope Wheel Lead Mining Centre. This opens daily from April 1st to October 31st between the hours of 10.30 am and 5 pm. For the rest of the year it is only open by appointment but school groups are making increased use of the centre during the off-peak period.

Killhope is alongside the A689 Stanhope to Alston road the latter being only 8 miles away and is in the county of Cumbria. Here then is one of County Durham's border and is one of the breeziest. Like Beamish described in Chapter 7 Killhope is developing all the time and those, like us, who make frequent visits are sure to find something new to marvel at. The huge water wheel which is 33 feet 6 inches high and once powered a crushing mill is again turning and producing a nostalgic grinding, squeaking and splashing sound. There is a very good audio-visual display, plenty of experts on hand, eager to answer questions, and many areas provide visitors with the opportunity to enjoy what these days have become known as 'hands on' displays. There are displays of mine workings, a typical lead miners' 'barracks' with lots of photographs to prove the authenticity of the displays. If such displays can be defined as relatively ancient then the visitors' centre and shop areas can be described as modern and efficient.

For those without cars, buses from both Alston and Stanhope run regularly on summer weekends thus proving that County Durham has now become an important tourist centre. The City of Durham itself also on the River Wear is obviously at the focus of this tourist trail. Durham is described in the next chapter.

CHAPTER 5

Durham City

There are two occasions on which to see the city of Durham at its best; during Advent when it is illuminated and the lights twinkle in the smooth waters of the River Wear. The other ideal time for a visit is on Sunday morning when the University students flock to the boathouses and take to the water.

There are great similarities between Durham and Lincoln, both of which have a castle and a cathedral perched on a hill overlooking a river and the two connected by a tangle of steep streets. Both are small cities well provided with reasonably priced car parks.

Durham is quite rightly classified as a World Heritage Site and the castle and the cathedral have an interwoven history because of the unique position held by the Prince Bishops.

The cathedral site is for ever associated with St. Cuthbert, but the hill overlooking the Wear has an even older history. There are signs in Old Durham of dwellings dated to the 1st century AD and the Romans were also present between the 2nd and the 4th century. It was not St. Cuthbert himself who established Durham as a religious centre but a married and initially very mobile group known as the Congregation of St. Cuthbert. They arrived in AD 995 and dropped roots in an area they considered to be safe.

In 652 St. Aidan died and it is said that on that night the young Cuthbert had a dream calling him to a religious life. The following morning he left his flock of sheep and walked into Melrose Abbey. He soon moved to Ripon where he became guest master. This was not the place for a young man trained by fervent down-to-earth Celtic monks and he soon fell foul of the more sophisticated Wilfred a devout believer in the ornate ceremonies typical of Rome. He returned to Melrose, soon becoming its Prior. In AD 664 he moved to Lindisfarne, becoming Abbot in 684. Cuthbert was as much a naturalist as a mystic and he died on the Inner Farne Island in 687. He was buried on Lindisfarne, also known as Holy Island Priory and which is fully described in our companion volume *Discovering Northumberland.*

Cuthbert's stone coffin was opened some twelve years after his death and his body was said to have remained fresh and it was thus suggested that a miracle had occurred. Such a body transferred to a richly decorated oak casket was bound to attract its share of rich and generous pilgrims and the abbey became wealthy. By 875 the abbey was providing welcome pickings for the Danes and the Lindisfarne Congregation of St. Cuthbert began their travels taking with them their grizzly assets. St. Cuthbert had to share his casket with the bones of other Saints including St. Aidan and the head of St. Oswald. They also took with them a number of valuable manuscripts including the famous illuminated Lindisfarne Gospels

The Congregation was kept continually on the move by the 'plunder hungry' Danes and they spent some time at Chester-le-Street in 882 and were then at Ripon until 995 when they found peace at Durham.

Their first building was of wood but later replaced by a church of white stone. This was later swamped beneath the magnificent Norman cathedral, but whilst the chapter house was being restored in the 19th century remains of the early church came to light. Also found were a number of Celtic crosses.

St. Cuthbert's followers decreed that their lands should be hereditary and this worked very well until the Norman Conquest. It was then that William I felt that he needed a reliable Norman in charge of this vulnerable border country and that he could not trust the Saxons or the Celts. He thus expelled the Congregation and appointed Bishop Walcher of Lorraine to look after Durham. Between 1071 and 1080 Walcher planned what has become the finest Norman church in England. The present hilltop complex has been accurately described as 'Half church of God, half castle "gainst the Scots"'. The mighty church was protected by the Norman castle on one side and on the other was the buildings of a Benedictine monastery.

Durham when viewed from the air can be seen to be one of Europe's finest cathedral cities.

Most cathedrals are usually entered quickly without wasting time gazing at the door, but Durham should be the exception. Although the present door knocker is but a replica since the original was removed to the safety of the library, as befits a 12th century relic. This is an example of a sanctuary knocker with the fugitive hanging on to it to gain safety. Construction of the cathedral was begun in 1093 and was largely completed by 1133, a remarkably quick period. Other significant buildings built after this period are the remarkable Galilee chapel finished in 1170 and the Chapel of the Nine Altars finished in 1242. A much later construction was the solid central tower built between 1465 and 1490.

There is a fine colourful guide to the cathedral to take the visitor around the building and there is also a well stocked shop and there would be little point in attempting to repeat this detailed information here. Our overriding memory of St. Cuthbert's church, however, is its simplicity with huge soaring pillars illuminated by light streaming through the magnificent rose window, and the Gallilee chapel.

If the church itself is simple, there is nothing simple about some of its furniture, the pride of place being taken by the Neville rood screen. This was funded by John, the Lord Neville from 1372 to 1380 and was brought from Caen in Normandy.

This wonderful complex of buildings is not only a church but also the most complete medieval Benedictine monastery to be found in England. The cloister garth is a particular joy with its well and lavatorium (a line of washing basins) situated close to the door of the refectory.

The Chapter House is also in excellent condition and was completed during the time of Bishop Rufus (1133-1149) and within it are the graves of the early bishops. Between this and the south transept Bishop Wessington (1416-1446) constructed a library which served until the 1680s. Dean Sudbury then converted the old Norman refectory into a library which was extended in 1854 by absorbing the huge dormitory. This extra space was certainly needed to house more than 50,000 volumes including some manuscripts dating from the time of Bede and the pre-Conquest abbeys of Wearmouth and Jarrow which are described in chapter 9.

Durham is to be commended upon its use of space, satisfying modern demands without compromising its history. The undercroft beneath the dormitory which was once used as cellars for the kitchen has now been converted into a book shop and a remarkably fine restaurant. The northern part of the undercroft which was once used as a common room for the monks has now been converted to house the Treasury holding St. Cuthbert's coffin and his followers' portable altar and cross. There is some Anglo-Saxon embroidery and examples of their elaborately constructed and coloured manuscripts.

The area of the Cathedral Close is known as the College and in the mid 17th century this almost became a University. Oliver Cromwell went so far as to appoint staff but the Commonwealth came to an inglorious end before any students were enrolled. In the event this had to wait until the 28th October 1833 and was due to the generosity of the Bishops of Durham who gave the castle to the new university, the third oldest in England. Initially it was purely ecclesiastical in its aims, but it has now become secular without ever losing its religious pedigree. To make way for the university the Bishops moved their palace to Bishop Auckland where they still are.

Thus the history of the University begins with the history of the castle and this is why we feel that Durham is unique. This is because of the Palace Green where the undergraduates and the visitors to the city mingle. We particularly remember enjoying a walk around the green surrounded by students doing their last minute revision before going in to the stifling cauldron of the examination room.

The castle is open only to official guided tours for which the University makes a small charge, but nobody keen to discover the history of the city can afford to miss the opportunity. Tours are operated on Monday, Wednesday and Saturday between 2 pm and 4.30 pm. Other opening times are posted on the entrance gates.

As we have seen already the castle is unusual in that it was built by churchmen but who also doubled as military men. There are still many early features including the line of the old dry moat across which stands the Norman gateway which has survived an 18th century attack by the restorer James Wyatt who refaced it. Still in position are the solid 16th century oak and iron gates which slam shut at night, but the students can still use a wicket gate to reach their rooms.

Durham Castle was never required to take on an active military rôle and within the well proportioned courtyard are a wide variety of undamaged architectural styles from early Norman to the relatively modern. All of these are described on the guided tour. There is a Norman undercroft chapel which dates to 1072. This was deserted and neglected for centuries but was restored in 1952 and has been used for worship ever since.

The advantage of having the University actually using the castle is that the building feels lived in. What was the

Bishop's dining-room is now the senior common room and its 16th century ceiling is a joy. The students of University College have their dining hall in the old Great Hall originally constructed over a Norman undercroft dating to the late 13th century and with substantial additions being made in 1350. The improvements included a musicians' gallery and there were two magnificent thrones. This reflected the Bishops' dual function as head of both state in the area and of the church. The only disruption to the life of the castle came during the Commonwealth Period (1650-1660) but the Bishops soon recovered and restored their buildings. Since its inception the University has added its own glory to the Great Hall and portraits of its founders and benefactors look down upon the dining students. Whilst looking for student accommodation in 1840 the authorities replaced the ruinous medieval keep, with an accurate replica.

Outside the private area of the castle used by the University there are many wonderful buildings set around the Palace Green. The castle dominates the northern area, the cathedral the southern section with the square completed by a range of buildings to the west and east best explored by leaving the castle gateway and strolling around keeping the open green on the left. Behind the wall on the right is the Fellows' Garden which was once used as a leafy hiding place for the hard working bishops. The first complex of buildings now housing part of the University Library are of great interest. Bishop Neville's Exchequer building was constructed around 1450 and served as court rooms. Very few changes were needed to adapt the building to hold the Sharp Library of very early printed books originally collected at Bamburgh Castle in Northumberland. This library is sometimes opened to the public as is Dr. Routh's library of rare books brought from Magdalen College, Oxford. This is kept in a room above the Sharp collection.

As the circuit of the Palace Green proceeds the name Cosin keeps cropping up and few Bishops can have done so much good work as this 17th century cleric. He established a library in 1669 which he hoped would be put to good use by both the clergy and what were described as the 'literate public'. Among the important books are the bishops' own annotated

St. Cuthbert's cross, a fine example of 7th-century Anglo-Saxon workmanship.

copy of the 1662 Book of Common Prayer brought out after Cromwell Puritans had been ousted.

Windy Gap is usually true to its name but is a very attractive route down to the river passing the old Grammar School built in 1661 and now used by the University Music Department.

On the opposite of the Green, is another reminder of Bishop Cosin with his almshouses of 1838 being a replacement for those of 1666 which still stand. This is now used as the Almshouses Cafe and Restaurant and the inscription on the wall states that Bishop Cosin's building replaced Bishop Langleys Song and Grammar School established in 1414.

Beyond this is the magnificent Abbey House with a Queen Anne facade which blends surprisingly well with the rest of the buildings on the Palace Green. Despite Alec Clifton-Taylor's displeasure of Abbey House we feel just for once at odds with his normally impeccable judgement.

From the green our favourite way down to the river follows Saddler Street and Fleshergate once the base of the local butchers and then onto Elvet Bridge. This was built by Hugh Puiset the Prince Bishop from 1153 to 1193. It originally had 15 arches, but only 10 are now visible. Originally around 16 feet (5 metres) wide but this was almost doubled in 1805 but it has never been anything other than a footbridge and thus ensured that its quiet leisurely atmosphere has never been disturbed. It is a marvellous spot from which to watch the river usually full of hard working 'serious' rowers. Just below the bridge, however, it is possible to hire a rowing boat whilst the pleasure craft *Prince Bishop* runs occasional cruises throughout the year and is for hire for discos and conferences.

Without doubt the best way to get to know the geography of a city is from its river and Durham is no exception with the *Prince Bishop* being purpose built and seating 150. In the summer there is plenty of room to sun yourself on the upper deck whilst on cooler days the vessel has a good central heating system.

The trip goes downstream as far as Maiden Castle, an important Iron Age Fort. Not much of this fort remains and it should not be confused with the archaeological more important Maiden Castle in Dorset. It does, however, serve to underline that the area was settled in prehistoric times.

From the *Prince Bishop* there are also fine views of the cathedral, castle and the city bridges, both ancient and modern. Naturalists will not be disappointed either, and on this stretch of the Wear we have watched dipper, grey wagtail, heron, several species of duck, including goosander and red-breasted merganser, with a kingfisher putting in a colourful appearance, near Elvet Bridge on a gentle summer afternoon.

Standing on Old Elvet Bridge an a hot summer morning is one of the tourists' pleasures as it gives plenty of time to explore its many facets. It leads to Old Elvet, a wide and spacious street, dominated by delightful Georgian buildings. Its glory is not even disturbed by the University Administration Offices or by the strangely attractive bulk of Durham top security prison.

Boating on the River Wear at Durham. The pleasure boat Prince Bishop is seen on the right.

Durham, however, is not just a fair weather city. In addition to the cathedral there are a number of fine churches to explore, and there are excellent museums, several of which are efficiently organised by the University. Some of these are of international importance rather than relating to County Durham in particular. Two in particular, however, are very relevant to students of the county these being the University Museum of Archaeology and the Durham Light Infantry Museum.

The Museum of Archaeology is delightfully situated on the river bank between Framwellgate and Prebends Bridge and is a wonderful place with only one major drawback. This is that there is no vehicular access, but it is only a short walk from the city centre. There is a nominal entry fee and the museum is open throughout the year. From April to October it opens from 11 am to 4 pm and from November to March from 12.30 to 3 pm. The building is below the cathedral and was once a fulling mill. Inside are displays concerned with the history of Durham City and its immediate surroundings, whilst temporary exhibitions are also held, thus ensuring that many visitors return again and again. There is also a Heritage Centre in the 14th century church of St. Mary Le Bow in the North Bailey which should be regarded as a supplement to rather than a rival of the Museum of Archaeology. It contains a collection of costume, visitors can try their hand at brass rubbing and the history of Durham is described in exhibits and a slick slide show. The Heritage Centre is a product of the 1980s reflecting a new interest in attracting tourists, whilst the Museum of Archaeology greeted its first visitors as long ago as 1833, but the staff have kept pace with modern methods of display. There is one very obvious advantage of a museum being connected with a university department and this is the provision of a direct link between scholarly excavations and the visitor. Here is the old Fulling Mill within which are displayed Roman and medieval artefacts with substantial material from the ruined manor house once the property of the medieval Priors of Durham at Beaurepaire, now known as Bearpark, which is around three miles to the west of the city. The area belongs to the council, and they have established a very pleasant picnic site.

The Durham Light Infantry Museum and Durham Art Gallery is about half a mile from the city centre on the A691 and close to the railway station. These days most visitors to Durham arrive by road, but our first few visits were by train. We would never dispute the oft stated belief that the approach to the city by train ranks with the best views in the whole of Europe.

The Light Industry Museum and the Art Gallery not only looks good but on summer Sundays it also sounds good as brass bands play in the landscaped gardens. Over the August Bank Holiday there is an annual rally of military vehicles of all ages and very impressive they look. There is an entry fee to the museum except on Fridays. It opens from Tuesday to Saturday from 10 am to 5 pm and on Sunday from 2 pm to 5 pm. It closes on Mondays except bank holidays. Inside are colourful displays tracing the history of the County Regiment between 1758 and 1968. Here are battle scenes to whet the appetite of anyone who ever played with toy soldiers, fearsome 'real' weapons, uniforms, drawings and photographs. The museum is not static and an impressive

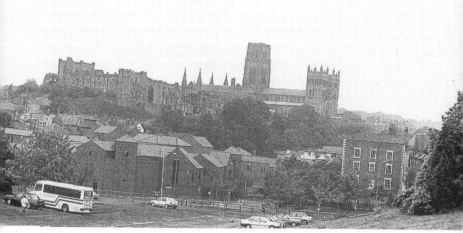

Durham castle (left) and Cathedral (right) dominate the city, being set on the crest of a hill over a loop in the river.

Medal room was opened in 1988. Also on display is a tank and a very solid looking armoured car.

This is however a War and Peace institution and on the upper storeys are exhibition galleries which are devoted to art of all periods and in which celebrated music recitals are held. There is a cosy coffee bar and great pains have been taken to cater for the disabled. The car park is extensive an important feature for a museum so close to the centre of a busy city.

Durham University has established an Oriental Museum which is open to the public at a very modest fee. It is the only such building in Britain to be devoted to Oriental art and antiquities and attracts visitors and students from all over the world. It opens from Monday to Friday from 9.30 am to 1 pm and 2 pm to 5 pm. On Saturday and Sunday it opens from 2 pm to 5 pm thus proving that it is not just aimed at the students. Of course such a museum has its obligatory Egyptian Mummy, but there are magnificent ceramic ornaments, delicate jade, impressive wall hangings, fragile Ming porcelain and a huge bed from China. This is a museum of contrasts and should be visited on the same day as the Light Infantry Museum. The terrifying Oriental weapons can then be compared with their more modern counterparts. There is an informative display describing the history of writing which should not be rushed and neither should the tour of the shop which sells some most unusual presents relevant to the collections.

Like any good university Durham caters for the scientist as well as the artist, and a visit to the Botanic Garden is a must, being open all the year round and having a modern visitors' centre with toilets, a shop selling souvenirs and a cafe. It is situated to the south of the city and has been skilfully planted on an 18 acre site near natural woodlands and sloping to the south west. As it matures the garden will become even more impressive with native British trees left in their natural position to provide shelter for the more delicate plants whilst the tropical species such as cacti are kept in glass houses. The garden is open from 10 am to 4 pm on 365 days a year and has its own car park.

Out of term time most of the Durham colleges offer tourist accommodation, details of which are available from the University Tourism Unit, Old Shire Hall, Durham DH1 3HP and this can be one of the best ways of discovering the city. For those who wish to have an informative whistle stop tour of the attractions then the best bet is to join a city tour led by one of the Blue Badge Guides. Details of these are available from the Tourist Information Office in the market place, itself an impressive area dominated by St. Nicholas church and the copper equestrian statue of the distinguished Victorian soldier, the third Marquis of Londonderry.

Since Silver Street was pedestrianised the ancient market place is seen at its best especially on Saturday when mobile stalls sprout in the early morning like magic mushrooms.

St Nicholas church is so impressive that it could almost be a cathedral in its own right. The north wall was built in Norman times and dovetailed into the city wall. After 'alterations' it had to be rebuilt in 1858 but the architect J. F. Pritchett followed a Neo-gothic plan and thus the church still blends in well with the old buildings of Durham. So does the town hall which is also Victorian but proves that not all work of that period is ugly. We feel that it may take a few hundred years yet before Victorian architecture is fully appreciated. The hammer-beam roof of the town hall is modelled on that at Westminster Hall. We were drafting this chapter in the summer of 1992, having just written a feature on the Preston Guild. Here in the west window of the Durham town hall we stood spell bound in front of a delightful stained glass showing the annual procession of the medieval guilds as they paraded through the streets and up to the cathedral. The present guildhall close to the town hall is a replacement for the 1316 building and some of the records and artefacts have been retained but alas the manuscripts of the mystery plays have been lost. What a pity that these could not be revived as at York because Durham is the perfect setting for such events.

On the outskirts of the City and set on a delightfully rural loop of the Wear is Finchale Priory which had close associations with the Durham Benedictines. The site on which the Priory stands is said to have been chosen by St. Godric in AD1110. He lived long enough to appreciate a good spot as he lived to be 105. He lived at Finchale in solitude for more than 60 years following a pilgrimage to Santiago de Compostella. The priory was begun in 1180 and was said to be popular with ladies who wished to conceive. All they had to do was to sit on a seat in the so called 'Douglas Tower' which 'had the virtue of removing sterility and procuring issue for any woman who having performed certain ceremonies sat down thereon'. Alas these 'certain ceremonies' are not recorded and in any event the power was lost following the Dissolution. Finchale was used in the main as a sort of rest home for the monks from Durham and looking at its setting it is still an excellent place to unwind. It is administered by English Heritage and set in the middle of a working farm where there is a small shop selling ice cream, postcards and guide books. We have been to Finchale many times, and have been alone, but on occasional weekends canoeing competitions are held. The car park then fills up and the attractive camping and touring caravan site is busy as competitors get ready to do battle with the white water.

The Wear twists and turns through a narrowing gap between limestone cliffs alongside which run attractive footpaths. The best view of the white water stretch of the river is from the wooden footbridge behind the shop. From the opposite bank there are ideal places from which to watch the river and photograph the abbey.

This, and Durham itself, soon disprove the view that the Wear is an industrial river. All of its upper and middle sections are spectacularly beautiful. Even the approach to the sea around Sunderland has its obvious attractions as chapter eight will prove.

Durham is an obvious base from which to explore nearby towns and villages including Lanchester, Esh, Kelloe, Pittington, Sherburn, Ushaw Moor, Witton Gilbert and Shincliffe.

Lanchester can be reached from Durham via 6 miles of old railway line forming yet another of the linear nature reserves typical of the county. Originally the line ran from Durham to Consett and was mainly used to transport iron ore and coal. Between Harbuck and Lanchester is the well named Accommodation Bridge. This was built to accommodate the wishes of farmers who were worried that the line prevented them moving their stock from one end of their land to the other as it had been cut by the line. A very tangible reminder of the old railway can be seen at Lanchester railway station which still stands.

The history of this large village goes back to Roman times as here was yet another of the forts built to protect Dere Street running from York to Hadrian's Wall. There is not much left of Lanchester Fort which the Romans called Longovicium - the long fort. This is because the fort was used mainly during the 18th century as an unofficial quarry. Several altars were thankfully saved, some of which are in the local parish church and others are on display in Durham Cathedral. What is left of Longovicium is not open to the public but it can be clearly viewed from the road to Satley. A pair of binoculars will enable the herringbone pattern on the stone to be seen. This patterning is more typical of Saxon architects, but perhaps they borrowed the idea from a Roman experiment!

All Saints parish church at Lanchester is rightly regarded as one of the most interesting in Durham and this is a particular compliment in a county so blessed with fine ecclesiastical buildings. Its sheer size and the quality of its furnishings prove that Lanchester was an important religious centre from Roman times, and some of the pillars from the fort are incorporated into the church. Remembered within is the Reverend William Greenwell a formidable archaeologist, historian, theologian and one time Canon at Durham Cathedral. He was not just a fisher of men, but also a fisher of fish and designed the fly named Greenwell's Glory.

All Saints was a collegiate church by the 13th century and continued to train priests until the Reformation. Both Norman and Early English architecture are well represented in the church. Lanchester is now a dormitory for those working in Durham and the industrial cities of the North East. There are still reminders of the coaching era represented by attractive inns and its former farming period returns each July at the time of the popular and substantial Agricultural show.

Between Lanchester and Durham is the ancient village of Esh perched above the Rivers Deerness and Browney and which takes its name from the old English for an ash tree. On the green is a venerable old cross said to mark yet another spot on which St Cuthbert's body was rested during its journey to Durham. The parish church has been altered over the centuries but still bears traces of its Saxon and Norman origins. Esh Hall, the seat of the Smythe family, was once an imposing 17th century residence but very little of the original remains and is now incorporated into a farmhouse. The gate posts remain as a rather forlorn testimony to the family which produced Mrs Fitzherbert the secret wife of George IV.

Kelloe just to the south east of Durham is a perfect example that beauty is indeed in the eye of the beholder. The visitor should ignore the signs of industry and think history. There are three monuments of great interest here. In 1822 74 miners were killed at Trimdon Grange Pit and they are remembered. Elizabeth Barrett Browning was not originally of Wimpole Street but was born at nearby Coxhoe Hall in 1806 and

Christened in Kelloe church. What a pity that the hall was demolished in the 1950s because in these days of tourism it would have made a grand memorial to her work and that of her husband. She is, however, obliged to make do with a memorial erected by public subscription in 1897. The Norman church is worth a visit especially because of the Kelloe Cross which tells the story of St Helena's vision of the Holy Cross and she is also seen warning an unwilling Judas Iscariot by brandishing a sword over him, until he dug up the cross with a spade! This is one of the most interesting crosses to be seen in Britain and there is a tradition that Canute, King of both Denmark and England, made a barefoot pilgrimage from Kelloe Cross to St Cuthbert's Shrine in Durham in 1017. Kelloe reminds us of Jarrow, not in physical appearance but in the way that religious treasures have survived despite industrial upheaval.

This balance between culture, Christianity, coal mining and countryside, social history and shipbuilding is typical of the whole of County Durham.

CHAPTER 6

The Derwent Valley

The Derwent rises not far from the Wear and is mainly a County Durham river and the South Tyne which drains Northumberland. For much of its course the Derwent is the boundary between the two old counties. We have again ignored the setting up of the new 'artificial' area of Tyne and Wear. The Derwent flows past the delightful village of Blanchland which is in Northumberland, and described in our *Discovering Northumberland* in one end and out the other of the Derwent reservoir, before swinging north past Allensford, Shotley Bridge, Ebchester, Derwentcote, Gibside and then onwards to meet the Tyne near the Metro Centre at Gateshead. There is an Information Centre at Shotley Bridge which is open all the year round and this along with another at Beamish ensure that the visitor is supplied with up-to-date knowledge of developments which are occurring in this area at a refreshingly swift rate.

The moorlands around the source of the Derwent are the haunt of the large and colourful Emperor moth whose larvae feed on the heather plants. In late summer these impart a purple haze to the contours whilst in spring the new shoots provide cover for nesting grouse, curlew, redshank, wheatear and lapwing. The female cuckoo keeps an eye open for the chance to remove an egg from the nest of a meadow pipit and replace it with her own.

The first substantial settlement along the river is Blanchland, an unspoiled picture postcard of a village with a long ecclesiastical history. Blanchland is set at the southern limit of Northumberland and on the County Durham border which is formed by the river itself.

Edmundbyers is just in Durham, situated close to the Derwent reservoir and dominated by its church from which extensive greens slope downwards. These are flanked by attractive houses. This is camping and caravaning country, many people being attracted by the variety of aquatic sports on offer on and around the reservoir. The Punchbowl Inn serves a variety of substantial meals and is popular with tourists and with locals which is a good sign. There is also a popular youth hostel in the village which was once itself an inn.

The church of St Edmund, from which the village takes its name, dates to 1150. It has a remarkable collection of woodwork within its plain exterior but much of this has been collected from other churches. A witch is alleged to be buried in the churchyard. The village was once much busier than at present and round about there are the remains of lead smelting mills.

An important turnpike passed through Edmundbyers and the old bridge built by the trustees still stands although it has long since been by passed. Edmundbyers is surrounded by ancient common land and about 11 miles away to the east is the hamlet of Muggleswick. Here can be detected the ruined walls of a refugium used by the monks from Durham Cathedral during the 13th century. The monks seemed to have had a number of rest homes for they also had Finchale Priory described in Chapter 5.

Like the more famous Kielder Water in Northumberland, the 3 1/2 mile long Derwent reservoir which opened in 1967, was constructed both to provide water for industry and as an amenity for tourists. Although not so highly developed as Kielder, which opened in the 1970s, Derwent can lay claim to having laid down the ground rules. County Durham's industries, especially those around Wearmouth, make good use of the water but sailors, anglers, picnickers, walkers and those interested in natural history are also provided for. The southern shore is occupied by Pow Hill Country Park one of our favourite walking areas hereabouts, along with the increasingly popular Derwent Walk Country Park near Ebchester described later. Even at the peak of the holiday season these areas never seem to be over-full and there are plenty of places to be alone with the wildlife which is increasing in diversity with each passing year. As the 1990s give way to the next century the wildlife of County Durham is set to enjoy its most productive period for more than a century.

There is another delightful Country Park at Allensford on the banks of the Derwent where there was obviously once a ford and which is about 2 miles from Consett. There is good parking and picnic tables here, a children's paddling pool and play area, toilets and a site shop with a warden on duty. This is popular with the local people who enjoy walking among the rich variety of trees. Here on a cold January morning we watched a flock of brambling fly in to feed with the chaffinches around a clump of beeches. In June we watched a pair of starlings feeding their young in their nest in a hollow tree. We get so used to seeing starlings breeding in towns that we forget that they were once rather an uncommon woodland species but with great intelligence which enabled them to adapt to life in towns keeping one step ahead of the hungry or playful cats. Other breeding species include magpie, great spotted woodpecker and tree creeper.

Although it was Consett which developed during the Industrial Revolution, all the early factories were concentrated closer to the Derwent at Shotley Bridge, now relegated to a mere suburb of Consett. Steel was made at Shotley long before any huge steel work polluted the atmosphere at Consett which only lost its last furnace in the early 1980s. In the 17th century a small group of German sword makers fleeing from religious and political persecution settled alongside the Derwent and forged iron to produce the weapons for which they soon became famous. A furnace of the type they used still exists about 4 miles to the east of Derwentcote and has been restored by English Heritage. There is a small but impressive exhibition on site. Here it is explained how this type of furnace produced high quality steel for the first time. The method eventually reached Sheffield and helped to make Britain the fulcrum of the Industrial Revolution. There is a good car park and facilities for the disabled. The museum opens between 10 am and 6 pm from April to September and there is a small fee. As Consett attracted the industry, Shotley Bridge set out to attract visitors to partake of its waters and for a short spell during the 19th century it became quite a popular spa. Industrialists made their money in Consett and their homes in Shotley Bridge and even at the height of heavy industry the railway line was said to be one of the prettiest in the country. It still is, although it is a long time since a train rattled through Queens Station but the Derwent Way is now a very attractive walkway bordered by trees and level enough to make walking, cycling and horse riding a joy. Cycles can be hired from Stanley and Consett. Even the ubiquitous rosebay willow herbs look attractive, their red flowers earning them the name of fireweed.

Apart from Shotley Bridge, the Derwent Walk also passes close to Ebchester, yet another area in Durham with a history dating back to Roman times. The town can be reached via the A694 but there is also access from the Derwent Walk via the picnic site and Information Centre. The original settlement around a fort, which the Romans called Vindomara, was built to protect the river crossing over which ran Dere Street the road from York to Hadrian's Wall. Binchester near Bishop Auckland was another fort on this route.

The modern name Ebchester takes its name from St Ebba to whom the 12th century church is dedicated At this time there was a mistaken belief that the ruins of the Roman fort were those of a 7th century monastery dedicated to St Ebba. We have no evidence to support the idea but wonder if Saxon Christian monks lived for a time in the Roman ruins. The church was built in early Norman times and many Roman stones were used during its construction. A pagan altar can be seen incorporated into the tower. Mains Farm was constructed on the site of a Roman fort and in the garden there are the remains of the bath house and a small museum.

Two other places provide an excuse for those who like their walks to be through history to take the trouble to follow the Derwent Walk. Leap Mill Farm at Burnopfield was an 18th century water mill now an organic farm which is open on Sundays. The setting is magnificent and refreshments are available.

Nearby is the Gibside chapel, one of the most interesting buildings in County Durham. Its typically Palladian architecture was designed by James Paine and was to be a mausoleum for the Bowes family. It is signed from the A694 and B6314 from Rowlands Gill which is about 6 miles to the south west of Gateshead. There is a tea room, picnic area, clean toilets and a shop. Run by the National Trust, Gibside is open daily from April to October between 11 am and 5 pm except Mondays unless it is a Bank Holiday.

Although the chapel was begun at the request of Sir George Bowes, it was not completed until 1812. It came under the wing of the National Trust in 1966 being given by the executors of the 16th Earl of Strathmore and Kinghorne. It is a pity that Gibside Hall is now a ruin and not open to the public. This was built in 1620 but substantially altered in 1750 and 1850 funded by the profits of coal mines owned by the Bowes family. The hall was also worked on by James Paine and the grounds landscaped by Capability Brown. The dominant feature of the old grounds is the statue of British Liberty perched on top of a 140 foot high column. The Bowes family have another more important claim to fame. Lady Elizabeth Bowes Lyon, the Queen Mother, is a descendant of the Bowes family whom we have already met in Teesdale. The chapel above the mausoleum has a three decked pulpit, an umbrella shaped sounding board, and much of the timber of the pews is of highly polished cherry wood. Gradually the National Trust are opening more of the grounds and from the walls are views of the ruined hall, the orangery and other estate buildings, with fringing columns of Turkey oak. The public are warned not to approach the ruins of the hall, which are in a dangerous state, but there is ample evidence to show what an elegant 19th century house of the well-to-do was like.

In 1990 Gateshead hosted the National Garden Festival and few people at that time accepted that the area deserved to be chosen. Even fewer appreciated the beauty of the surrounding countryside. It is to be hoped that this book and others like it will add to its reputation. It now has a world famous athletics track and the New Metroland boasts that it is the largest indoor theme park in Europe. This is a good day out for those who love family fun and it is usually busy as it is easily reached from the A1(M) and from Newcastle-upon-Tyne via the Metro-Link. The Metro-Centre is a huge and comprehensive shopping centre built on reclaimed industrial land conveniently close to the A69. The centre is popular with the local people as well as travellers from the north of England and from Norway, the latter arriving by ship to Newcastle. They find the prices of clothes in England very much cheaper than in Norway, On a well planned shopping spree they can save more than enough money to cover the boat fare.

Gateshead developed from the 14th century onwards because of huge coal deposits and heavy industry, especially shipbuilding, which also developed along the Tyne. The church of St Mary is of medieval origin but was substantially and almost unrecognisably altered during the 18th and 19th century. This is excusable as local businessmen sought to improve their church.

In 1814 the first river steamboat in England was built at Gateshead and many others were later constructed. In 1878 a local man who became Sir Joseph Swan invented the incandescent electric lamp. Although it is hard to imagine these days that Gateshead, now dominated by towering blacks of flats, was once set among attractive riverside and wooded country. Here for a time lived Thomas Bewick who was born near Newcastle in 1753. Bewick was one of the first and finest of our naturalists and artists and his woodcuts are still much loved and sought after. To the south east of Gateshead is Windy Nook Nature Park which is a delightfully refreshing area to walk and very close to the town. On summer days slow worms can often be seen basking in the sun.

Such havens for wildlife are becoming ever more common around County Durham and in a few years time it will be interesting to read the works of Thomas Bewick and compare the species he describes with the modern list. We have a feeling that we may be pleasantly surprised.

CHAPTER 7

Around Chester-le-Street and Beamish

Many people, perhaps with some excuse, have never felt the need to discover Chester-le-Street. During 1991 and 1992 we met several people who had never heard of the town until Durham was admitted to the cricket county championship and set about establishing their headquarters in the town. Once at the heart of County Durham's coal field it is now recovering from the industry and its beauty, which has always been there for those with the persistence to search, is shining through.

Chester-le-Street has an illustrious history dating back to Roman times. The word 'street' indicates the Roman road from Brough via Binchester to the bridge over the Tyne known as Pons Aelius. We now know this as Newcastle and to the Romans Chester-le-Street was called Conganium. Here the Romans built a now long-vanished fort and around it there developed a vicus, or civilian settlement which provided essential services. In return for providing its essential service industries the vicus was provided with protection by the fort.

The settlement, although deserted by the Romans when they were obliged to funnel back to protect their doomed empire, continued to be used by the Saxons. In the 9th century the coast of Britain was under almost constant threat from the invading Danes. Some of these incursions were described in our companion volume *Discovering Northumberland* and we noted that the body of St. Cuthbert had to be hastily removed from Lindisfarne and carried inland, a story which we continued in the chapter on Durham in this present volume. Before finding its eventual resting place at Durham, Cuthbert's body 'rested' at many places includ-ing Chester-le-Street where it remained from 883 to the 990s in an area close to the old Roman fort. There was a wooden church here for more than a century until Cuthbert's followers moved off first to Ripon and then finally Durham.

A vintage Blackpool tram still operates around Beamish. Even on a wet day this is a splendid museum.

Had Cuthbert's body not been moved a massive cathedral would no doubt have been built at Chester-le-Street and would have become the centre of Northern Christianity rather than Durham. In the late 11th century Bishop Egelric decided that a splendid church should be built at Chester but whilst the foundations were being excavated a valuable horde of Roman coins was discovered. The Bishop, for obvious but sad reasons, abandoned the church and went back to his old haunts at Peterborough with the loot. He did not get away with the deed, however, and was imprisoned on the orders of William the Conqueror. A church was actually built at Chester-le-Street during the 13th century and despite a number of insensitive restorations, particularly during the 19th century, much of the original structure can still be seen. Inside there is a fine collection of 14 tombs of medieval knights. The spire, completed at the turn of the 15th century, is acknowledged by experts on ecclesiastical architecture as the finest in Durham. St. Mary and St. Cuthbert has parts dating to 1056 and its story is told within the Anker's House Museum, entry to which is free. It is open daily, except Sundays, between April and September from 10 am to 4 pm.

The museum is constructed on two floors and describes how an Anchorite monk was walled up for life with his food pushed in through a small hatch. Presumably excreta was passed out via the same contact with the outside world but the monk's life has to be considered as one of unproductive contemplation. The museum also has artefacts dating to the foundation of St Cuthbert's church of AD 883 almost up to the present day.

As one would expect of a town with such an ancient church, Chester-le-Street had an important market and open air stalls are still a feature on Tuesdays and Fridays. The pattern of the old town set at the junction of the Cow Burn with the Wear remains with its expansion halted first by the A167 and then the A1. It had a period of importance as a coaching stop off the Great North Road and it was also on the main rail link, the centre of the town huddled beneath a colossus of a viaduct.

If the medieval church deserves to be celebrated then so, up to a point, does the ultra-modern Civic Centre, a modern attempt to emulate the Crystal Palace. This is a brave attempt to make local government less intimidating and there is so much light within that 'indoor' trees grow very well and a pleasant little restaurant is part of the complex.

Chester-le-Street is still a pleasant little town despite some inroads made by industry, and is seen at its best from the Riverside Park. Across the river are two magnificent looking castles but only one is genuine. Lambton Castle was built by the Lambton family beginning in 1794 and continuing there until 1932. Since 1900 there has been more demolition of the 'mock castle' than new construction but it is still mightily impressive. Among the ruins there are many reminders of the work of a number of influential architects including Joseph and Ignatius Bonomi and Sidney Smirk.

In contrast Lumley Castle is genuine and dates to the 14th century. It has been largely left alone but the impressive eastern front and some impressive interior work was designed by Sir John Vanburgh. The building is now an up-market hotel with its own golf course and popular with travellers along the nearby Al(M). Regular Elizabethan banquets are held with a wonderful atmosphere created by the original castle turrets, but it is not usual for Lumley's white lady ghost to appear. The Lady of Lumley remains firmly a part of folklore but is definitely not a fact!

Chester-le-Street has its share of streets built for workers and also villas built for the newly rich of the Industrial Revolution, but to discover what life was like in the working centre of county Durham, a visit should be made to one of the best museums in Europe which is situated at Beamish.

We had visited Beamish several times before we appreciated its real contribution to the Tourist Industry not only of Durham but much of the North of England. On a grey day of sweeping rain we realised what a wonderful asset Beamish is not only to the tourist but also to the serious historian.

The North of England Open Air Museum has a massive car park and well behaved dogs are allowed in on a lead. From April to October the hours are 10 am to 6 pm each day whilst in winter it closes on Monday and shuts at 5 pm. Whatever the season there are no admissions allowed after 4 pm. The entry fee includes all transport and exhibits. This makes Beamish sound like any other theme park, but it is actually much more than this and apart from the fun provided this is a serious and well organised museum.

Outside the entrance is a very well appointed Information Centre and in Beamish itself a large shopping complex and the first of a series of well appointed toilets. The museum is set among 260 acres of rolling meadows and woodlands criss-crossed by the Beamish Burn, an attractive little stream haunted by both grey and pied wagtail as well as a number of herons. Just inside the entrance of the museum we climbed aboard a vintage tram and from its upper deck we could see a heron ignoring the sweeping rain, and greedily feeding on earthworms washed out of their burrows by the floodwater. Beamish has several working trams, with others being repaired and the oldest in use is the Blackpool No 31. This was built in 1901 by the Midland Railway Carriage and Wagon Company. The eighty-six seater was almost completely rebuilt in 1918 and then ran in Blackpool until

The Shepherd and Shepherdess public house in Beamish village.

1934, but remained in the engineering works of the town until 1984. It then came to Beamish to be restored in its original livery.

In 1907 the Preston Electric Car Company constructed Sheffield's tram number 264 and the fifty-nine seater was in use until 1956 and this too has been carefully and accurately restored. It is also possible to travel aboard a 1925 Gateshead tram which carries 48 people and on the single deck tram originally from Oporto in Portugal and built in the 1930s but to a design dating to around 1910. Whichever tram is chosen the visitor is transported back through time as well as space to the Town, a very real and living history with the year 1913 being chosen as the focus. The Town is typical of a north eastern market town of this period and some buildings were brought from Ravensworth Terrace, Gateshead.

This is no mere museum piece even though the buildings have been brought from elsewhere and re-erected brick by brick. The correct furnishings have been selected but the difference is that at Beamish they are 'staffed' by 'residents' with the right knowledge and accents. Fires burn in the hearths and the costumes are authentic. Here is the working home of a solicitor, a lady music teacher and a dentist. Here we saw his foot drill, gas apparatus and a frightening collection of instruments. This was of particular interest to us as one of us worked as a dental technician during the 1950s and this place reminded us of the surgeries and workshops which were only being phased out during the 1950s.

There is also a shopping centre, the focus of which is the Co-operative Store brought from Annfield Plain and which was built in 1873. The present shop has been furnished as it would have been in 1913. Once again this is an accurate trip down memory lane, the Co-op being the complete discount shopping centre with each customer's purchases being entered in a book and every so often a percentage discount was paid and known affectionately as 'the divi'. We can both remember going down to the Co-op for the 'divi' and watching the family order being collected. Sugar was weighed into blue bags, butter cut from the barrel and skilfully patted into blocks. We can also remember the central cash collecting system linked by an overhead tube which carried money to the office and brought back change and receipts. This Lamson-Paragon system is still in working order in the Co-op drapery and hardware area. There is also an insurance department which meant that the shop could look after its customers from the 'cradle to the grave'.

Above the Co-op is a well stocked and realistically priced cafe called the Dainty Dinah Tea Room. Opposite is a newspaper office and above this a fully operational print works typical of 1913 and which still prints some leaflet for the museum. It is possible to buy note paper printed here and provides a good opportunity for visitors to buy unusual presents. Next door to the print works is a 1913 style pub called the Sun Inn which still works and serves drinks and bar snacks. What a pity that the prices are of the 1994 vintage and not 1913! Behind the pub are working stables with splendid dray horses in comfortable residence.

There are colourful tin advertisements everywhere in the town but especially on the short steep road down to the small railway station which really does look authentic despite being a jig-saw of artefacts and engines brought from all over the North East. Regular steam hauled journeys are a feature of Beamish. Once again the illusion of 1913 has been faithfully recreated to produce a branch line typical of many in the district which were operated by the North Eastern Railway. As explained elsewhere in this book, the railway system evolved in the North East, the earliest lines associated with the transportation of coal from the numerous pits to the seaports or the sites of heavy industry. Many of the old stations have closed and the skilful workers at Beamish have brought buildings and artefacts and stitched them together to produce a realistic station.

The station building itself was built in 1867 at Rowley near Consett and this was brought brick by brick to Beamish. This was a comparatively easy construction task as the station never had gas or electricity but was lit by oil lamps a feature which has, as usual with Beamish, been faithfully retained. The cast iron footbridge was removed from Bunston and dates to around 1870 and the 1896 signal box came from Carr House East close to Consett. Another iron footbridge from the same period was brought from Howden-le-Wear near Crook.

From the town a working replica of a 1913 Daimler omnibus runs a continual shuttle service to the pit village which has been constructed with the same loving care as the town. On the way to the Pit Village we looked down at the fairground which despite the rain on the day of our visit was full of happy children whose laughter could be heard even over the electronic music from the restored carousel which dominates the area. Here also are a colourful set of swing boats, a coconut shy and a round of flying chairs. We returned two weeks later on a warm summer Sunday and listened to a brass band playing at the bandstand in the Town Park.

The miners were very fond of brass bands and also of their allotments, pigeons and whippets. All these activities have been copied in and around the Pit Village and Beamish still organises whippet races and leek shows. From the bus stop in the yard of a coal mine set-up we joined a group of fellow tourists, donned our hard hats and followed a guide, dressed as a 1913 miner, some 80 yards into a drift mine. We were

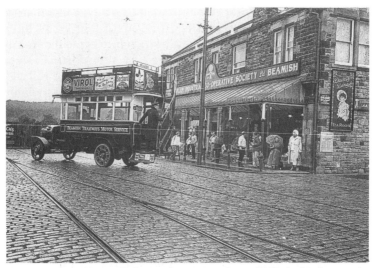

The 'Town' at Beamish features a copy of an old Daimler bus and a rebuilt Co-op store brought brick by brick from nearby Annfield Plain.

treated to a wonderful account of the life and times of a hard working Durham miner and his often large family.

There are two ways of extracting coal from underground seams - by deep shaft mining or by drift mining which was simply a horizontal tunnel hacked into a hillside. Drift mining actually went on at Beamish from 1850 and only closed in 1958. When we entered the Mahogany Drift Mine we were in no doubt that we were walking into history. Drift miners could use naked lights because they were operating so close to the surface that they were well ventilated and there was no time for the build up of the explosive methane gas to occur. Miners could therefore use candles or - if they could afford to buy one - a carbide lamp. Again the museum staff play their part and our guide looked and sounded like a 1913 miner and his carbide lamp burned with a hot, bright, flame which brought back happy memories for us. We come from a family of iron ore and copper miners and as methane gas is also unknown in these workings we remember carbide lamps just after the Second World War. As children we helped to crush the carbide which was then placed in the bottom of

The interior of the Co-op store at Beamish.

the lamp. Water was then gradually dropped onto the carbide from an upper chamber, the flow controlled by a tap. The chemical reaction produced acetylene gas and it was this which was burned. Carbide lamps were used in the pits and also on the bicycles which were the main mode of transport to and from the pits.

In 1913 miners were comparatively well paid and face workers had 38 shillings (£1.90) per week but they also had free coal and a rent free cottage. They did, however, have to

Inside a dental technician's workshop at Beamish.

provide their own mining tools except for the wooden pit props which the owners provided. The work was physically hard and accidents, often fatal, were frequent. At nearby West Stanley in 1909, 168 miners were killed including 60 boys. Some small effort was made to ensure safety underground which was the main job of the pit deputy who could be identified by wearing a leather cap and carrying a stick which he used as a measure to check the safe distance between the pit props. He went underground before the men and when

The miners' cottages and allotments at Beamish.

he thought the mine was safe he waited at his station and met the men on their way to their own seam. The deputy had a box at his station in which were kept details of the diggings and the rudimentary rescue equipment. All miners were on strict piece work. During an eight hour shift, the hewer hacked coal often from drifts of less than four feet high and it was then shovelled into tubs which were pushed out from the face into roads. In each tub the hewer placed his personal tally which enabled his wages, which were paid fortnightly, to be calculated. The tubs were moved along the road either by children called putters or by ponies also driven by children who were called pony putters. These unfortunate youngsters were paid by the number of tubs they moved. A good hewer and his putters worked very much as a team and paused only to eat their meals which were referred to as bait.

What little time the miners enjoyed above ground they used to the full and tended their gardens, hens and bred rabbits for food. They flew pigeons and raced whippets whilst the wonderful leeks which they grew were far too important to eat and were shown proudly in hotly competitive shows.

A miner-guide deep inside the drift mine at Beamish.

The whole of the North East was once covered in a rash of small pits and villages composed of small houses were built around them. Those reconstructed at Beamish came from Hetton-le-Hole and were built in the 1860s and once formed part of Francis Street. They were lived in by miners and their families until 1976 but they have been reconstructed to look as they would have been in 1913. The only variations are that one house has been set up as a study area for school parties, and another as the colliery office, a not unusual event around small mines. In the cottages themselves, coal fires burn and heated the ovens in which bread is baked and smells wonderful. Mangles stand and tin baths hang in the back yards which have wash houses and long drop earth closets. Inside the dim interiors lit by oil lamps are furnished with heavy carved furniture which seems to have been hacked from solid wood and designed to last much longer than one generation. We remember our mining grandparents' cottage, which was almost identical to those at Beamish and we enjoyed talking to the 'residents', some of more than 250 staff employed at the museum. Like most miners our families were solid in their Methodist faith, sang rousing hymns, the ladies joined in the Bright Hour and the children went off

The railway station at Beamish was brought from nearby Rowley.

scrubbed clean as a pin to the Sunday School. At Beamish Museum a Wesleyan chapel has been brought from the nearby village and in 1992 a Board School which was originally built at East Stanley in 1892 has been erected next to the chapel. Not only have the staff got the furnishings of the school right but it also smells right. Each class-room has seating for around 50 pupils and ink wells and pens and text books lie around as if awaiting the monitors to distribute them. The schoolmaster wanders round with his shiny boots and high winged collar. In the 1890s he picked out the brightest of the children and allowed them to instruct the younger pupils. The walls and cupboards reflect the teaching, with geography concerned with the British Empire, the science dealing with chemical, physical and grizzly biological experiments. English concerned itself with grammar and classical literature, the mathematics taught by means of the abacus, the computer of its age, and tables learned by rote. Standards in 1913 were high and the teachers dressed in the manner of solicitors or eminent physicians, deserved and demanded respect.

The more people employed in the pits and the larger their families the more food was required and Beamish has its own farm, part of which was in a dilapidated condition when acquired by the museum during its early days in 1972. Once again the 1913 theme has been followed and even the livestock are being selectively bred to produce the stock present on the farm of the time. Cheese is produced and sometimes sold, the ovens produce bread and pies as the farm and its kitchen come to life. The Durham Shorthorn cattle are still here and were once famous throughout England, being herded along well marked drove roads leading to the lucrative markets of southern England. The Durham Ox has given its name to many hostelries along these ancient routes. The Durham Shorthorn was an all purpose breed which provided both meat and milk. By 1913 the transport system had improved to such an extent that even villages did not have to be totally self-sufficient. Stores like the Co-operative developed their own factories and farms or brought in bulk so that they could reduce prices. This was really the beginning of our modern supermarket system.

The area around Beamish, whilst it shows many scars of industry these are fast healing and the countryside is increasing in beauty. At Beamish village itself, which is less than a mile from the museum, there is much to see including the fine Georgian inn with figures over the door to represent 'The Shepherd and Shepherdess'. This hostelry serves excellent bar snacks.

There is a footpath leading from the museum to the famous Causey Arch but this is best reached by road. It is surrounded by a country park, which is provided with plenty of parking, picnic tables and good toilets. From the car park the Arch is signed along a narrow twisting path lined with flowers and in August we listed wood sage, harebell, foxglove, herb bennet, blinks, Enchanters nightshade, Himalayan balsam and toadflax.

Causey Arch is something of a mecca for industrial archaeologists as it is the world's earliest railway bridge. The concept of railways was realised as early as 1640 when horses were pulling carts along wagon ways. As the Durham mines developed it became increasingly vital to carry their coals to

Newcastle from where it was transported by sea to towns and cities including London. A group of coal owners who became known as the 'Grand Allies' combined to fund railway tracks from their mines around Tanfield and found the huge gorge cut by the Causey Burn to be an impossible obstacle without the construction of an embankment and a bridge. In 1725 they employed Ralph Wood to design a bridge to breach the 80 foot gorge at a height of 100 feet. With no other bridge existing Wood based the single span on an ancient Roman design. The architect had so little faith in his stone structure, probably because his wooden prototype collapsed, that he is said to have committed suicide by jumping off the Causey gorge before the bridge was finished. Ralph Wood need not have worried because his arch has survived as one of the wonders of the early days of the Industrial Revolution. There was a huge explosion at Tanfield Colliery in the 1780s which resulted in its closure but thankfully the bridge was not demolished and remains as a link between Roman and modern civil engineering.

Railways in the area, obviously including the Stockton-to-Darlington, developed apace in Durham especially in the Tanfield area and a glimpse of these early days can be gained by a visit to the nearby steam railway. The line operated as early as 1725 with horses pulling coal wagons along wooden tracks. A route ran from Tanfield to Gateshead at first including the Causey section but this was modernised in the mid 1830s. The wooden tracks were replaced by metal rails and the horses by stationary steam engines linked to wires and pulleys. The stationary engines were not replaced along all sections until the 1880s but eventually the Tanfield area was linked to the British rail network until its closure in the 1970s, an event precipitated by the exhaustion of the Durham coal fields. Enthusiasts are at present rebuilding two sections of the line and are already contributing to the growth of tourism in the area. The section from Sunniside to East Tanfield including the Causey line is now working. The trains are reached by following the signs from Stanley and in the summer months regular trips run as far as, but not crossing Causey Arch. This is by far the best way for the disabled to reach the arch and the viewing platform above it. The

Causey Arch is the oldest railway bridge in the world, and is based upon a Roman design.

alternative route from the Causey Arch picnic site is rather rough, undulating and quite muddy after rain. Near the arch is a typical wooden wagon and a section of reconstructed wooden rail. Below in the valley the Causey Burn is still polluted by run off from the old mine workings, but it is still a beautiful place for a picnic.

Steam trains run every Sunday from April to November from 11 am to 5 pm and also on Thursdays, Saturdays and

The Tanfield Railway — one of County Durham's developing tourist attractions.

Bank Holidays during the school vacations. The station and sidings are on view throughout the year and there are occasional special events such as Santa Claus specials for children. The line can also be hired for private functions.

Some idea of the extent and importance of the Durham coal field can be gained from visits to Beamish, Causey Arch and the Tanfield railway and further information can be gleaned by visits to Stanley and Consett.

Stanley is a breezy upland town which has worked hard for its living and has paid a heavy price, for it was here that on 16th February 1909 the explosion occurred in the West Colliery which killed the 168 men and boys a sad event mentioned earlier in this chapter. There is a memorial to them in the churchyard. Mining, some of it open cast around Annfield, has proved to be resilient and here is another connection with Beamish for it was from here that the Co-operative store was transported to the museum. It will take time for the full effects to be noticed but many of the old spoil heaps have been grassed over and are already popular with wildlife. Of special interest is Harperley Country Park, set in the wooded valley of the Kyo Burn and here we watched a female redstart feeding her young which were almost ready to fly out of the nest set in the hollow of a rotting tree.

Consett was once an important steel town, but little now remains of the massive complex of furnaces which once worked day and night. Industrial it may have been but there were few finer sights than Consett when the molten slag was tipped and lit up the sky with a vivid red. The fortunes which turned a village into a town began around 1837, Queen Victoria's Coronation year, when large local deposits of coal and iron ore were discovered. In a short time up to the 1890s the population rose from 200 to more than 10,000 and there were soon souls to fight for. It was here that the first Salvation Army band tuned up and burst into brassy melody in 1879. Once the mining industry had gone Consett became almost a ghost town and only began its recovery in the 1980s.

The town is surrounded by a network of redundant railways many of which have been or are being laid out as country parks. These are described in a series of leaflets produced by Derwentside Leisure Services and on sale at local information centres. Three within easy reach are the Consett and Sunderland Railway path, the Waskerley Way and the Derwent Walk.

The Consett and Sunderland Railway path was constructed and is still being developed by Sustainable Transport, a charity intent upon opening up traffic free routes in the area. There are many parking areas along the linear route of $11^{1}/_{2}$ miles of old track decorated at intervals by so called environmental sculptures. This produces a unique stroll along one of the oldest railways in the country. Cycles can be hired from Beamish, Stanley and from Consett and there is also a bridle path running parallel to the main track. There are several pubs and cafes along the route and the surface has been specially strengthened and is ideal for wheelchairs. The line was once used to transport iron ore and other materials. Apart from the man made metal sculptures including Durham Shorthorns cattle there is one very solid reminder of the Consett steelworks. The crucible was used to carry molten metal during the manufacture of steel and now stands above the track. Children use it as a fascinating and unique climbing frame. John Downie wrote a fascinating novel of this area called *The Celestial Railroad* and several quotes from this have been arranged at intervals along the route.

In contrast the Waskerley Way is not suitable for wheel-chairs along the whole of its length, but there are gentle stretches approaching the Crucible at Berry Edge and at Rowley Station Picnic Area. The old station, as we have seen, has now been re-erected at Beamish. Again there are pubs and picnic areas along the route and cycles can be hired at several points. This is mainly a moorland track but it passes close to Waskerley, Smiddy Shaw, Rowley and Castleside reservoirs which combine to produce excellent bird watching apart from the warm summer months.

Waskerley village is now almost ghost-like having had the character ripped out of it when the railway was closed. Here were once engine sheds, repair works and houses, a church and a school for the workers and their dependants. A few houses are still occupied and served by a small post office.

Another interesting spot is known as Nanny Mayer's Incline named after a lady who once kept a nearby moorland tavern. The horses had to work so hard to pull the wagons up from Hounsgill towards Waskerley that they were put into 'Dandy Carts' and given a ride back down the hill. Obviously these days have long gone, but a more tangible reminder of the old days is the Hounsgill viaduct built in 1858 by the Stockton and Darlington Railway Company to carry wagons at a height of 150 feet above a ravine.

Yet another old railway is followed by the Derwent Walk which was described in chapter 6. The tracks and also the wonderful displays at Beamish show how quickly the industrial scars of County Durham are being healed and put to good use.

CHAPTER 8

Around Hartlepool

Although Hartlepool is now part of the county of Cleveland it should, in our opinion, still be an integral part of Durham as it developed as the principal port for the Prince Bishops. Here were collected the customs due from oil, wines, copper and tin, all of which were imported in quantity. At the same time there was a flourishing export trade in lead, corn, cloth and even people. The Cathedral of Durham had the right to grant sanctuary to the oppressed and many were allowed to leave the country via Hartlepool.

It was the Saxons who probably established the first religious house here in the form of the monastery of AD 640. Its main claim to fame was as the training ground for the Abbess Hilda who became the second to hold office at Hartlepool before moving off to Whitby there to establish one of the most famous houses in Britain. Hilda followed the Benedictine Rule and as was the custom of the time the abbeys were 'mixed' and used by both male and female followers. Hilda is still commemorated at Hartlepool in the name of the parish church, but nothing remains of the monastery founded by St. Aidan on the Headland and which flourished between AD 640 and 800 before being destroyed by the Danes.

St. Hilda's dominates Old Hartlepool standing proud on the headland over the bay with houses clustered around its squat tower. This was built around 1250 and is supported by half a dozen solid buttresses. Inside there is a long nave made up of seven bays supported by a cluster of columns constructed around 1200. The clerestory is also magnificently built and throws shafts of light into the body of the church. So well did W. D. Caroe restore the decayed East End of the church that it is hard to distinguish between his work of 1924 from the 13th century original. Behind the High Altar is the tomb of Robert Bruce who founded the church. The family were Lords of the Manor here and at the village of Hart from

St Hilda's church at Hartlepool is an ancient site among both new and old houses and warehouses.

the 11th to the 14th century being also known as de Brus. Their most famous member was another Robert Bruce who became King of Scotland.

In 1189 the powerful Bishop of Durham had a fleet built at Hartlepool for the use of King Richard I, and in 1201 King John granted the town its charter. During the wars between England and Scotland Durham, as we have seen, acted almost like a buffer state. Especially during the reigns of Edward I, II and III Hartlepool was of great importance and the harbour was a sanctuary for the English fleet and the town market used as a vital focus for supplies. Edward I was rightly called the Hammer of the Scots but his son (Edward II) was much less able and in 1314 he sailed into Hartlepool following his defeat by Robert de Brus at Bannockburn. How ironic it must have been that the town had been founded by his victors' family. In 1315 the Scots followed up Bannockburn by sweeping through the town and inflicting considerable damage.

It then became obvious that Hartlepool needed its fortifications strengthened and the town and its equally vulnerable harbour were enclosed behind solid walls. Little of this medieval wall remains but enough can be seen at Sandwell Gate to give some idea of its strength.

Hartlepool must have recovered well from the visitation of the Scots because in the 1530s it was affectionately described as 'the best of any haven town in England' but it did not maintain this position in the centuries which followed. Perhaps the vessels increased in size and found access to the harbour more difficult or perhaps the harbour became silted up. It was probably a combination of the two but in any event by the mid 18th century there were proposals put forward to fill in the harbour and use it for growing crops. In the end it was the coming of the railway which saved the port. With the opening of the Stockton to Darlington railway a spider's web of tracks spread out into Durham and by 1835 the rich coal fields were linked to the port of Hartlepool.

During early Victorian times the new town of West Hartlepool grew up around the port, and shipbuilding and marine engineering developed to provide the needs of the coal exporters. A new coal dock opened in 1847 and in its first six months 54,000 tons of coal had been exported in 460 ships. This led to rapid expansion and by the 1890s West Hartlepool was the third busiest port in England behind London and Liverpool. It was certainly the dominant port on the North East coast and in 1882 there were 66 shipping companies owning around 200 vessels many of which were built in West Hartlepool This figure had risen to 240 by the year 1912. By this time shipbuilding had also became an important industry and the new town was a complex of cranes and the noisy machinery associated with heavy industry. The most famous firm was Sir William Gray and Company who built the first oil tankers and between 1878 and 1900 won six Blue Ribands for the best output from British shipyards. It is no wonder that the Germans sought to inflict damage on the West Hartlepool shipyards and others on the north east coast. In December 1914 there were many civilian casualties when the Headland came under heavy fire from a squadron of five of the Kaiser's warships. These ships also inflicted some damage along the coastline of Yorkshire around Whitby and Scarborough and which we described in *Discovering Coastal Yorkshire*. Later in the war the town came under attack from zeppelins. The gritty response was to increase the number of yards.

At the end of the war it was only natural that the demand for new ships would decline rapidly and the Hartlepool yards came under great economic pressure, but Gray's yards survived. During the Second World War there was no shortage of work but in the slump which followed Hitler's defeat, even Sir William Gray and Company failed to overcome the depression and 125 years of engineering excellence came to an end in 1962.

Hartlepool always seems to have been able to keep its historic element separate from the industrial area and could really be considered as two towns. The two Hartlepools – Old and New – are thus both well worth discovering.

Many other areas with fine shipbuilding traditions completely turned their backs on their traditional skills but not Hartlepool. The docks have become famous for their restoration of old ships including the Royal Navy's first ironclad warship *HMS Warrior* which was built in 1860 and was then taken to Portsmouth where it is on display. She was built on the Thames and was the largest, fastest, best protected vessel of the period. The literature on sale in Portsmouth is most complimentary regarding the restoration carried on by the shipwrights of Hartlepool.

Hartlepool itself is set, during the 1990s, to become a Maritime Exhibition Centre in its own right with a museum and a collection of ships including the *Wingfield Castle* and *HMS Trincomalee*. These are both based at Jackson Dock which along with the Coal Dock and West Harbour, has been designated a marina area with berths for more than 400 leisure craft and a complex of new houses, offices, light industry and tourist attractions. The project looks like becoming an invaluable amenity in the area during the 1990s and into the next century.

The *PSS Wingfield Castle* is a paddle steamer built in 1934 by Sir William Gray and Company to ferry cars and passengers across the Humber between Hull and New Holland near Grimsby. Her sister ship the *Tattershall Castle* is anchored on the River Thames in Central London where

HMS Trincomalee is being restored at Hartlepool at a cost of between five and seven million pounds.

she is used as a floating restaurant. The restoration of the *Wingfield Castle* has been expertly done in the original livery colours of the 1930s London and North Eastern Railway Company. This consisted of a black hull, white superstructure and a bridge made from best quality teak.

The vessel now known as *HMS Trincomalee* was built in 1817 at Bombay and is the only surviving example of a Napoleonic Leda class frigate. Both the *Trincomalee* and the *Wingfield Castle* can be toured on weekdays between 2 pm and 4.30 pm and on Saturdays and Sundays and Bank Holidays between 10 am and 4.30 pm on payment of a small fee.

With two such fine ships, Hartlepool could well become self satisfied with its place on the tourist map, but with its reputation assured as a centre of excellence for ship restoration there is always likely to be new things to see and is therefore a place to return to again and again.

Two other places which should be visited are the Gray Art Gallery and Museum on Clarence Road and the Maritime

The Wingfield Castle paddle steamer is being restored at Hartlepool where she was built.

Museum on the Headland two miles from the Town Centre and which is wall signed.

The Art Gallery and Museum was presented to the town in 1920 by the shipbuilder William Gray. There is a large and fascinating collection of 19th and 20th century oil paintings and there is also a comprehensive display of local social history and world wide archaeology. Of no relevance to the area but very interesting nevertheless is the Japanese Gallery and Oriental collection which includes a fierce looking Samurai warrior.

There are also areas devoted to local geology, natural history and especially relevant is the display devoted to marine biology. The grounds are an important extension to the museum and there is a reconstructed electric tram office, the Cerebos 'nodding donkey' pump once used to raise brine from which salt was produced and the village smithy transported from the nearby village of Hart. Entry to the Gray museum is free and opens Monday to Saturday 10 am to 5.30 pm and Sunday 2 pm to 5 pm except Christmas Day, Boxing Day, New Year's Day and Good Friday.

The Maritime Museum is also free but does not open on Sundays. Here is reflected the town's connection with the sea including fishing, an early gas-lit lantern from a lighthouse, a mock-up of a fisherman's cottage, and exhibitions of shipbuilding and marine engineering. The siting of the museum helps the visitor to see what is happening in areas of dockland which are still working including the Deep-water Berth, the Fish Quay and the Fabrication Yard. There is a simulated ship's bridge and a very important collection of ships' models.

Around Hartlepool are a number of what were once little villages in their own right, but have been absorbed by the developing town. Included are Seaton Carew, Greatham, Elwick, Hart, Dalton Piercy and Newton Bewley.

Seaton Carew was once a tiny fishing village which grew as Hartlepool grew providing the hard working artisans from the shipyards with a seaside resort. Prior to this wealthy Quakers from Darlington had used the area as a 'lung' and built imposing villas and shops sprang up to serve them. In 1783 a twice weekly coach ran from Darlington and the first hotel was built in 1793 but it was in Victorian times that the real development took place. Now there are many typical seaside amusement arcades sandwiched between Seal Sands and the industrial complex of Hartlepool. Seal Sands may well have been just that prior to the Industrial Revolution but they have long been swamped beneath oil tanks, storage globes, gantries, pylons and security fences. Just to the south at Port Clarence is the Transporter Bridge crossing the Tees to Middlesbrough. Seaton Carew Sands is an oasis among this industrial sprawl. A path runs along the edge of the golf course and continues to North Gare Breakwater from which a wild stretch of dunes leads to a spot from which shipping can be seen entering and leaving the River Tees.

Greatham is pronounced Greet-Ram and derives from the Old English 'Great' meaning stoney ground and 'Ram' meaning village. It straddles a ridge of sand and most of the village is now designated a conservation area. Here again we have an oasis of a village this time sandwiched between the heavy industry of Billingham and Hartlepool. The long winding main street leads to the parish church and a building known as the *Hospital of God*. The church of St. John the Baptist was largely and not too carefully rebuilt in 1855 with a west tower added in 1909. Inside there is plenty of evidence of the late 12th century building itself built over an Anglo-Saxon structure. Evidence for the latter was found when the 1909 tower was being constructed and bits of Anglo-Saxon crosses were unearthed. The altar is made of Frosterley marble which rests on two baluster shafts dated to the late Saxon times. Both the church and especially the *Hospital of God* received funds from Robert de Stichill who in 1272 was Bishop of Durham. Like the church this complex has also been rebuilt since it was established as a hospital. A hospital did not have the same meaning in those days but was a place where old and infirm people were given hospitality. Bishop Stichell's Alms' Houses were refounded in 1610 but the main buildings date to the late 18th century. The building was designed by Jeffrey Wyatt (or Wyatville) and his work was funded by the Duke of Bridgewater in 1803. The building is a solid structure of stone with a rather taller central hall with a courtyard on either side. It is topped by an impressive bell tower. The hospital is now the home of old and ill clergymen and their well-being is looked after by the 'Master' who is also the vicar of the parish church. The Hospital Chapel was rebuilt in 1788 but contains some interesting remnants from the original chapel. There is an altar slab and a brass inlaid tombstone of one William of Middleton who was the Master of the Hospital in 1312.

Close to the Stitchill's Hospital is another set of Alms Houses, the Dormer Parkhurst Hospital, founded by 'Master' Parkhurst in 1762. The row of brick single storey cottages is now home to four widows or 'unmarried sisters' who must be over 50 and in need.

The Greatham Hospital Trust still owns the bulk of this attractive village and the Master lives in Greatham Hall which was substantially rebuilt in 1962 but has a distinctly Georgian feel about it and has retained one 18th century room almost in its entirety. Here was the home of Ralph Ward Jackson, the founder of West Hartlepool.

The lighthouse and cannon overlook the coast at Hartlepool.

For those who enjoy watching traditional village ceremonies, then Greatham has two dates for their calendar. On June 24th the Feast Day of St. John the Baptist is celebrated and on Boxing Day the area echoes to the sound of the Greatham sword dancers performing outside the church gates.

Elwick is rightly famous for its delightfully situated church which has Saxon origins proved by carvings on each side of the chancel arch. The church overlooks a village whose main street separates two greens and which lies off the A19 which links Sunderland and Stockton-on-Tees. The nave of the church is 13th century as are the aisles, with the chancel dating to the 17th century but the tower is only 19th century but it was built with sufficient care to look much older.

Hart also has a magnificent church and was the mother church of the old port Hart-le-Pool. The name derives from the Saxon word 'Heorst' which means a stag. The church, as at Elwick, has Saxon origins and this can be detected by a close examination of the fabric. It is now dedicated to St. Mary Magdalene, but was originally dedicated to St. Mary the Virgin.

Most of Hart church is Norman and after the Conquest Henry 1st granted the Manor of Hart and Heortnesse to Robert de Brus II in 1106. During this period the family were very powerful but prior to the Conquest the Saxon manor was even larger and included Billingham which is now swamped beneath a complex of chemical works.

As you stand on the church car park you should remember that you have a foot on a bit of British (not English) history for beneath is much of the Brus Manor House. Only a section of the wall remains above ground level but this is a listed monument. Look to the north of the church where there is a damp hollow, all that remains of the medieval fish pond a most valuable item in the days before refrigerators.

There are a number of buildings which the discoverer should seek out especially the Hart windmill, two public houses, and the birthplace of a Derby winner – the horse not the jockey!

Hart windmill is just to the south-east of the village and was probably built in the late 18th century, but on the site of

Souter lighthouse near South Shields has been restored by the National Trust who also own the surrounding coastline.

other mills dating back to the 13th century. It is hoped that the mill which last ground corn in 1915 may soon be restored.

The Raby Arms and the White Hart Inn both have interesting histories. The Raby Arms obviously had connections with the Dukes of Cleveland who lived at Raby Castle described in chapter 2. At one time, not too long ago, many hostelries brewed their own beer and opposite the Raby Arms the old brewery building still stands.

The White Hart has a wooden figurehead on its wall thus keeping alive the seafaring traditions of the Hartlepool area. It is said to have been salvaged from the wreck of the barque *Rising Sun* which was based at Sunderland. In a great storm of 1861 more than 60 ships were wrecked in Hartlepool Bay. We wonder where the other 59 figureheads ended up!

Just to the south of the church is a cottage called 'Voltigeur' which was once the stable of a horse of the same name which romped home first in the 1850 Derby.

There is still some splendidly exciting natural history in the area with Hart Bog supporting some important plants and insects and has rightly been declared a Site of Special Scientific Interest. Hart Warren Dunes bear a similar distinction and here are found greyling, common blue and Durham argus butterfly whilst the reptiles found include common lizard and the slow-worm.

Dalton Piercy is also of interest to the naturalist and just to the north is a wooded valley called the Howls and here breed the common redstart, tree pipit and the spotted flycatcher. There has never been a school, or a public house or even a church in this village. Despite these flaws it is remarkably attractive, and known to have been occupied in the 13th century but what is seen today is mainly 18th or 19th century set around a spacious green on which the lift pumps still stand. This is a pretty spot and so is Newton Bewley which derives its name from 'Beau *lieu*' which means a beautiful place. Like Dalton Piercy the village is concentrated in two rows of buildings which include cottages, farms and hostelries, the latter once serving travellers following the old main road to Hartlepool. The old village windmill is worth searching out although this has been converted into a private dwelling.

This ancient form of energy generation is somewhat upstaged at the Hartlepool Energy Information Centre which is well signed from the centre of the town and entry is free. It is based in Hartlepool Power Station which is open six days a week. There is what is termed a 'Generations of Energy' a voyage of discovery of the history of electricity generation. There are video presentations, working models, computer graphics and cameras linked into the working power station. Hartlepool is nuclear powered and great pains are taken to stress both the safety aspects and cleanliness of this type of generation.

From Hartlepool there is an interesting and at times surprisingly attractive route northwards to Sunderland via Castle Eden Dene and Seaham. Beyond Sunderland, Whitburn, Souter Point and Marsden Rock lead to South Shields and Catherine Cookson Country which is described in the final chapter.

Close to the coast is the unusual town of Peterlee, a new town which in 1948 was named after Mr. Peter Lee who was the first Chairman of the Labour controlled Durham County Council. Notice was taken of the damage done to the old towns of County Durham by unwise planning and here are open green spaces and landscaped slopes which are a delight. It is only two miles from the sea and this is overlooked by

Castle Eden Dene Nature Reserve which is one of our favourite spots. This 500 acre (200 hectare) reserve is administered by the Peterlee Development Corporation and is at its best in spring and summer although on one golden autumn morning we watched both red squirrel and badger feeding on the fungi which grows on the damp valley floor. The narrow valley slices down from an upland plateau of magnesian limestone down to the shingle beach and beyond this the sea. This is one of the great unspoiled areas of the Durham coal field despite being sandwiched between Blackhall and Easington Pits.

Botanists looking at the geology of the area believe that the natural climax vegetation would be ash and yew, but for many years oak has been planted probably because of its value as shipbuilding timber. In the early 19th century a ship was built from oak of the valley and appropriately called the *Castle Eden*. There has also been some planting of non-native trees including sweet chestnut, sycamore, rhododendron, hornbeam and a number of conifer species and these have thrived next to native species including alder, wild cherry and bird cherry, holly, hazel and hawthorn, blackthorn and elder. The variety of flowers is if anything even richer and include dogs mercury, bluebell, primrose, cowslip, wood anemone, lily of the valley, round leafed wintergreen, giant bellflower and a surprisingly rich variety of orchids including bird nest, early purple and fly orchid.

As one would expect from such a rich botanical carpet, the variety of insects can be breathtaking including the Castle Eden argus butterfly and several interesting moths such as barred carpet.

As County Durham becomes more environment conscious even the coal port at Seaham can be an exciting place for bird watching especially in spring and autumn following equinoctial gales. The birds can be watched from the harbour which is still busy as coal is tipped down chutes into the holds of ships which are almost 50 feet below. The harbour was funded in 1828 by Lord Londonderry and is still privately owned. In 1993 the future of both pit and harbour were threatened. Seaham is very obviously still a mining village but it has now turned one eye towards the potential

Marsden Rock and the Grotto on a summer afternoon.

of the tourist industry and there is plenty of parking overlooking the harbour. On the outskirts of the village is Seaham Hall and opposite this is a country park with plenty of free parking and toilet facilities. There are grassy footpaths running along the cliff tops and here we watched fulmars sailing on stiff wings over the North Sea whilst enjoying our picnic among the harebells and bloody cranesbill. Steps lead down to the surprisingly clean beach.

Close to the winding wheels of the colliery, Seaham Hall, now a retirement home, has its place in literary history. It was here in 1815 that Lord Byron married Anne Isabella Milbanke, the niece of Lady Melbourne but alas their union lasted less than a year.

At one time there were many mines situated inland from Seaham but most of these have long since closed and those which still work extract coal from deep seams beneath the North Sea. The church of St Mary the Virgin is more than 900 years old and has seen its share of tragedy. In 1962 the local lifeboat capsized and all the crew were lost, but an even greater loss of life occurred in 1880 when 164 miners died not to mention 181 pit ponies who also perished in the explosion.

We have visited Seaham many times and on each occasion we have noticed less industrial pollution and more to please both the locals and the tourist. The same may certainly be said for the area around Sunderland which now boasts its autumn illuminations. These should not be treated as a joke but as a very serious and successful attempt to show that Wearside has valid pretensions as a tourist attraction. Sunderland, once the largest shipbuilding town in the world was able in 1992 to celebrate its elevation to the position of a city with its polytechnic raised to the level of a university.

Before exploring Sunderland itself some time should be spent around Washington with its strong American connections and important Wildfowl and Wetlands Centre.

High an a hill close to Washington is the Penshaw Monument now owned by the National Trust and built in 1844 by George Lambton, the first Earl of Durham. It is a copy of the Temple of Heseus in Greece and despite its incongruous appearance it has settled well into the landscape. The family has another place in the folklore of County Durham – the Lambton worm. This is supposed to have been a fearsome dragon which terrified the local population and it was so long that it could wind itself nine times round Penshaw hill. Another suggestion is that it wound itself around Worm hill but wherever it was it is a member of the Lambton family which slew it! The family ought to have got rid of it because it was one of their sons who caught a 'warm' as the locals pronounced it. It was so small that he threw it into a pond. He then went off to fight in the crusades. Whilst he was away the 'warm' grew into a dragon and caused havoc. On his return Lambton consulted a witch and struck a bargain. He was allowed to slay the monster on condition that he killed the first person he met after so doing. With the deed done the young man met his father and did not carry out his promise. Legend tells us that the next nine males in the family all met untimely deaths!

Washington New Town was created in 1967 and its population of around 80,000 has flooded into around a number of small villages without entirely drowning their character. Here among the plants of Nissan UK and Dunlop and the offices of the DSS is Washington Old Hall run by the National Trust and which always seems to be overflowing with American tourists in search of the ancestors of their beloved 'George'. On the 4th July special events are always held and on this day the New World is certainly dominant over the old. The American link is not so strong as many suggest and whilst the hall belonged to George Washington's relatives, there is no proof that he ever visited the Old Hall. He resided at Sulgrave in Northamptonshire. The hall about 5 miles west of Sunderland off the A19 and only 2 miles from the Al, is open daily between April and October. There is a fee and the hall opens between 11 am and 5 pm with the last admission at 4.30 pm. Between 1183 and 1288 Washington was the home of George Washington's direct ancestors and the family retained ownership until 1613. Parts of the house are 13th century but there were a substantial alterations made in the early 17th century possibly after the Washingtons left. There are, however, many reminders of the family and one room is devoted to their history and many souvenirs are on sale. The Old Hall was in such a poor state that it was almost demolished in 1936 but it was then restored and has been in the caring hands of the National Trust since 1956.

If you have to build new towns then Washington is the way to do it even though visitors can be confused by the American-like trend to sign areas of the town as Districts followed by a number. Many houses are set on the bank and above the River Wear which is surprisingly clean these days. This is proved by the rich bird life found around the Wildfowl and Wetlands Centre which is in District 15 and signed off the A195 and A1231. It is also reached via the River Wear Ferry which runs from Sunderland.

Washington is one of eight national Wildfowl Centres, the others in the chain first established by the late Sir Peter Scott at Slimbridge in 1948 being Caerlaverock in south western Scotland, Martin Mere, Welney, Arundel, Llanelli and Castle Espie. Washington is open daily from 9.30 am to 5 pm in summer. It closes one hour before dusk in winter and does not open at all on Christmas Day and Boxing Day. There is good parking, toilets, children's play space, a picnic area, exhibition area and a gift shop.

The area of just over 100 acres (40 hectares) follows the usual pattern of the Trust reserves with enclosures of captive birds, feeding stations and hides placed around ponds and reed beds which attract wild species. These are at the best in winter when wildfowl and waders are both varied and abundant. Washington caters well for disabled visitors and many of the information labels are duplicated in braille and tape recordings are available. Because there are so many different species Washington, like all the other centres, is an ideal place to begin the study of birds. Visitors should not forget that these reserves have a vital role in the conservation and breeding of endangered species.

Close to Washington are two very interesting museums, the 'F' Pit Museum and the North East Aircraft Museum. In the hey-day of coal mining there were more than a dozen pits around Washington the only reminder of these days being the 'F' pit museum on Albany Way in Washington District 2. In conjunction with Beamish this is the place to discover the history of mining in the North East. The centre piece of the museum is the steam winding engine built in 1882 and capable of lifting 120 tons of coal per hour from a depth of more than 700 feet. It still operates when visitors request it but these days it is turned by electricity.

The North East Aircraft Museum is run by a knowledge-able group of enthusiastic amateurs and based behind the new Nissan factory which was built on the old Second World War airfield at Usworth. When the car factory was planned the museum had to move and now its situation may seem to be out of context. On display and visible from the car park are several vintage aircraft including the Canberra, Vulcan, Super Sabre F100, a Lightning and a F84F Thunderstreak. There are also helicopters including a Wessex and a dragon-fly. As Unsworth was a Second World War fighter base the World War II uniforms, photographs and artefacts on display are entirely relevant.

Transport is also the theme of the Bowes Railway in Springfield village. This is the only remaining standard gauge railway which was rope hauled and built to carry coal from the mines to the Wear. It was first operated in 1826 and some parts of it are the original work of George Stephenson although later sections were added in 1842 and 1855. At this time the line was 15 miles in length and visitors to the complex get a realistic impression of what it was like when working. Steam hauled rides are available and there are guided tours, a shop, exhibition and a refreshment room.

And so to Sunderland – poor underrated and too often undefended Sunderland. Instead of following the 1930s guide books which describe the town as dirty and ugly, visitors should take a good look at the sights of the new city as well as the beaches and coastline which surround it.

Before the industry came to what is now Sunderland there was three distinct settlements. On the southern bank of the Wear were Bishopwearmouth and Sunderland (meaning the south land) whilst the north bank was dominated by Monkwearmouth, one of the most important Christian settlements in Europe. Whilst the mouth of the River Wear has been a significant part for upwards of a thousand years it was only from the 1870s that the shipyards achieved such dominance that they were second only to the Clyde in output. The works can be seen from the famous Wearmouth Bridge built in 1928 and which replaced an equally famous bridge of 1796.

This was featured in the Sunderland Lustreware Jugs, produced by the Sunderland pottery which operated between 1807 and 1865. The pottery was painted with a metallic film which when fired gave it an iridescent glaze. The bridge was almost always featured on the jug but often with a verse beneath or around it. Examples of this famous ware can be seen in the Museum and Art Gallery on Borough Road. This is open daily free of charge. Here is an ideal place for a wet day visit of discovery as it describes the history of the area including shipbuilding, coal mining and the manufacture of glass culminating in the production of Pyrex. There are many models of ships and in the wildlife gallery is an interesting aquarium. There is plenty of culture on offer including paintings by L. S. Lowry, Burra and J. W. Carmichael. Wallace the Lion, however, is still the star exhibit so far as children are concerned. Equally fierce looking is

The Grotto is now one of County Durham's most interesting hostelries.

the display of the armour and weapons of a Japanese Samurai warrior.

In the mid 19th century with dock space at a premium, artificial docks were constructed and Sunderland had one further advantage over its competitors – George Hudson, the railway king, became MP for the town in 1845. In the following year the Hudson dock was cut out of solid lime-stone and the railway links developed. On North Bridge Street is the Monkwearmouth Station Museum which has hardly been altered since it was built in 1848 and closed in 1967. It is now a super museum with rolling stock including a guard's van dating to 1915, an Edwardian booking office and lying about looking ready for the next train are luggage trunks, a porter's barrow and other artefacts. Bicycles are also part of the complex.

Another museum dealing with social history is the Grindon Museum on Grindon Street and this also brings Edwardian Sunderland to life by recording the every day life in a shipbuilder's house. There is a model of a cook at work in the kitchen, a child in its nursery as well as a sitting room and a bedroom. A similar set up to Beamish is created here but without the living models. The museum has a dentist's surgery, post office and a cobbler's workshop.

On the north side of the Wear is the oldest and most historic part of Sunderland – Monkwearmouth. These days the monastery of St Paul's at Jarrow gets most of the pilgrims and it is often overlooked that this was only one of a twin foundation and was not even the oldest. Monkwearmouth was the mother house founded in AD 674 by Bishop Biscop. In AD 681 ten monks and twelve novices travelled 7 miles north from Wearmouth to set up Jarrow under the guidance of Ceolfrith. Again the impetus was provided by Bishop Biscop who persuaded King Ecgfrith the King of Northumbria to give land. St Peter's church therefore stands on one of the most important early Christian sites and its foundation is recorded in the writings of the Venerable Belde. The present church stands in a large open space close to a clutter of declining industry, but the situation is still attractive as the church overlooks Sunderland harbour. It retains some Saxon masonry including walls and the west tower with some contemporary windows. Pevsner describes this as 'a precious relic in a sordid setting'. It is still precious and the setting is nowhere nearly as sordid as it used to be. The history of the site is well explained in the Information Centre within the church.

The Sunderland area now deserves to be considered as a potential holiday area especially at the time of the illuminations and before moving further north three further places should be visited namely the Ryhope Engines Museum and Pumping Station, Hylton Castle and the Fulwell Mill.

Ryehope is between Sunderland and Seaham and the Engines Museum which is well signed is run by a charitable trust. There is a well displayed and humorous exhibition of vintage toiletry but it is the water pumping engines which are the focus of the exhibition. They were built in 1869 by Hawthorns of Newcastle and until 1967 pumped 3 million gallons of water each day from the wells beneath to supply Sunderland. The magnificent machines which cost £9,000 were fully restored in 1970 and can occasionally be seen working, when steam is generated especially on Bank Holiday weekends.

Both Hylton Castle (on the A1231) and Fulwell Mill (on the A1018) are on the north side of the Wear. Hylton Castle was built about 1400 but experts feel that its architect working for William de Hylton, created a home more for comfort than for defence. It did however once command a crossing point of the Wear. It could perhaps be that the building was a gate house and the strong castle behind it may have vanished. In the 18th and 19th centuries the Bowes family added lateral wings and it is now managed by English Heritage. Inside there is a display of medieval heraldry and there is said to be a resident ghost of the Cauld Lad who was a stable boy cruelly murdered by one of the early de Hyltons.

Fulwell tower mill on Newcastle Road dates to 1821 and is a stout solid structure built of local limestone. It is one of the best preserved windmills in the North East thanks to the efforts of the Tyne and Wear Industrial Monuments' Trust although it has not been used for serious milling since 1949.

Beyond Sunderland are the twin resorts of Roker and Seaburn. Roker pier is the northern arm of Sunderland harbour but its sandy beach is popular with anglers, sun bathers, swimmers and wind surfers all of which ensure that the inshore rescue team have to keep a wary eye open. There is plenty of car parking here except when Sunderland Football Club are at home at nearby Roker Park. Few grounds can be sited so close to the North Sea and with a gale blowing the players will have need of all their skills. Worth investigating is the Sunderland Volunteer Life Brigade Nautical Museum based in the Watchhouse. The museum was founded in 1877 and inside are records of local shipwrecks, the mariners rescued, ship figure heads and an impressive collection of photographs. St. Andrew's church is modern but in its own way as impressive as other more older establishments in the area and described by Sir John Betjeman as 'a bold and imaginative experiment which has triumphantly succeeded'. It was designed by Sir John Priestman who was not an architect but a shipbuilder and he completed the church in 1907. Its impressive furnishings include a carpet designed by William Morris and a tapestry by Burne-Jones.

Roker and Seaburn share two miles of sandy beach with the usual collection of seaside amusements, cafes and bars. At Roker there is a crazy golf course, a boating lake and the

Seaburn Centre has a play park with a theme heavily concentrated on blood thirsty pirates. The holiday feeling is reinforced at Whitburn where there is good swimming and beyond it is the Souter Lighthouse and Marsden Bay. Whitburn's sloping green is surrounded by attractive stone built houses and the tree-lined streets belie the fact that this was once a colliery village. The church is interesting and much 13th century work remains especially in the early English tower. It has, however, been substantially restored since. On the surrounding cliff tops is Whitburn Bird Observatory, entry to which is by permit. It was set up with the intention of recording the movements of seabirds and passage migrants. There is free access to the footpaths around it however, and here in winter we have watched snow bunting, shore lark and on one freezing January morning a Lapland bunting our one and only sighting of this species.

Along the cliffs near some disused lime kilns is the entry to the National Trust car park serving Souter Lighthouse and the Leas. The neat lighthouse painted red and white and reached via a grassy track from the car park, was built in 1871 and was one of the most advanced lights of its age. It is open on payment of a fee between April and October daily except Mondays, unless it is a Bank Holiday, from 11 am to 5 pm. The last admission is at 4.30 pm and there is a large shop and Information Centre. It is possible to visit the Engine Room, Buttery Room and Light Tower from which there are wonderful views across the North Sea. The fog signal station is also open and there are excellent display panels. There is a small cafe, toilets and a picnic site. The Leas is a large open area of grassland running along the coast and from this there is excellent birdwatching and the plant life is also impressive.

Between the Leas and South Shields is our favourite bird watching area in the North East. Marsden Rocks has everything – steep cliffs at the foot of which is a pub, a flat clean beach and a small island used as a seabird breeding ground. From the large car park steps lead down to the beach and the pub but the latter provides a lift for its customers. Excellent bar snacks are served but we prefer to watch the birds before eating.

The top of the Marsden Rock, which has had a 100 foot high arch punched in it by centuries of battering by the sea, is the breeding ground of a colony of cormorants.

Other species breeding around the cliffs of magnesian limestone are kittiwake, fulmar, herring gull, a few pairs of lesser black backed gull and rock doves the ancestors of the town street pigeon.

After our birdwatch we usually return to the Marsden Grotto pub for a meal and on a good day we can sit outside and continue our watching from the comfort of the seats. This is a particularly good vantage point in the spring and autumn when migrating birds pour through the area.

The Grotto was built by Jack the Blaster, a miner who in 1782 literally blew holes in the cliff to provide a home for his family. He soon found that he could earn extra cash by selling drinks to inquisitive visitors. Round about 1812 Peter Allen, a gamekeeper once in the employ of the Marquis of Londonderry, took over and extended the grotto into a 15 roomed tavern which became the base for a notorious gang of smugglers. They fought the excise men and also among themselves if we are to believe the tale of John the Jibber. It is said that John betrayed some of the smugglers to the authorities and he was tried by the band, found guilty and suspended from the cliffs in a wicker basket until he starved to death. His ghost is said to haunt the grotto and the management leave a glass of beer out for John the Jibber each night. They tell us it is always empty in the morning!

One thing which is always full is the children's buckets loaded with fine soft sand and the birdwatchers' notebooks whatever the season. Whenever we visit this area we always seem to end up at Marsden Grotto, one time haunt of Jack the Blaster and John the Jibber! This is the stuff of novels and so is the final chapter of this book. South Shields is Catherine Cookson country, the haunt of one of the best selling authors of the 20th century.

CHAPTER 9

South Tynedale — Catherine Cookson Country

Katie McMullen was born in a small flat on June 20th 1906 in Leam Lane, Tyne Dock in the district of South Shields. She was the illegitimate daughter of Kate Fawcett and brought up by her grandmother and step-grandfather whose name she took. We now know this poor little lass as Catherine Cookson. She went to school at St. Peter and St. Paul's school in Tyne Dock but left at the age of 14, first to go into domestic service and then to work in the laundry of the local workhouse which stood on the present site of South Shields General Hospital. She worked hard and eventually travelled to Sussex to manage a laundry. The poverty of her early life made Katie McMullen both industrious and careful and in 1929 she bought a boarding house. In 1940 she married one of her boarders, a schoolmaster named Tom Cookson, a very happy union although unfortunately childless. It was not until 1950 that the first Cookson novel was published, but what joy she has given her readers ever since. Her novels are mainly set in her native north-east and the Cooksons came 'home' in 1975 and have become a local legend. The local authority have set up the Catherine Cookson Trail which identifies areas of her real life and others concerned with her fictional works. On a fine August Saturday we began by discovering South Shields before moving northwards via Jarrow and Hebburn.

South Shields is a vibrant blend of ancient Roman settlement, port, market town, seaside resort and busy shopping centre. Many of the streets have now been pedestrianised. The settlement initially grew around the Roman fort of Arbeia built at the mouth of the Tyne as an integral part of their defensive network facing the sea. Now set among a substantial housing estate the complex is open throughout the year and entry is free. Troops may have been present here as early as AD 80 when most buildings were of timber construction. During the AD 120s Arbeia was still

The rebuilt gate house of Arbeia Roman Fort at South Shields.

mainly of wood, but its importance around AD 163 was realised and resulted in many stone structures being constructed. Around AD 210 the Roman campaigns in Scotland meant many new buildings were required in order to service the troops and a substantial settlement would have developed around it. There was almost certainly some use made of the area following the Roman retreat and the fort may have been the birthplace of Oswin, an early Northumbrian king.

In 1875, after South Shields had become an important colliery town and bore the scars of its exploitation, some effort was made to excavate the fort. Another serious effort at excavation began in 1949 and in 1953 a museum was opened. In the late 1980s an ambitious project was completed as a full sized gateway was built following the precise pattern of the Roman plan. This is the only such structure to be reconstructed on its original site and very impressive it is. In the museum are many household and military artefacts plus a variety of fascinatingly carved tombstones.

South Shields has a number of good car parks - many free - and has an impressive town hall from which the local government of the area is organised. This is surmounted by a weather vane in the form of a sailing ship. The modern town, however, developed partly as a colliery site and partly as a Victorian holiday seaside resort and surprisingly this combination works. Near the new town hall is an attractive pedestrianised walkway through the shops to the old market

The market-place at South Shields with the old Market House in the background.

square. The market place is a delight with the temporary stalls serving fruit, flowers, footwear and fish, sausages, shoes and soap, hats and hamburgers, crabs and crockery, all sold with splendid good humour. One side of the cobbled square is dominated by the Old Market Hall built in 1768 and the other by the ancient church of St Hild (not St Hilda's as often quoted). Market days are Monday and Saturdays with a flea market the feature of each Friday. St Hild's church never fails to remind us of Norwegian internal architecture. The present church only dates from 1790 and has a splendid Georgian gallery but there has been a church here since AD 647, when St Aidan founded a monastery. A Northumbrian princess, named Hild, was chosen to supervise the affairs of the establishment. As with the majority of religious houses on the North East coast St Hild's fell foul of the Viking invasions. It was replaced first by a Saxon building which now lies below the nave of the present church which probably has its origins in early Norman times, being mentioned in a charter of 1154. It was also mentioned in a charter of 1204 during the reign of King John. A priest is first mentioned in 1256 when Walter of Jarrow was in charge

The interior of St Hild's church at South Shields.

at St Hild's which was still governed from Jarrow as it had been since the time of Bede. In 1322 the Prior of Durham decreed that Jarrow should appoint a 'perpetual chaplain' instead of having to make an annual appointment. Although there have been several rebuildings some of the medieval church remains and can be found by those with time to explore the church.

St Hild's is a church with a difference because immediately you enter the building there is a lovely smell of fresh coffee and confectionery from the cafe to the right. To the left is a small information centre and a book stall. This gives a rather theatrical atmosphere which is continued as you pass through the doors into the church, which is full of light and colour. It is this Scandinavian appeal which surprised us. It was probably the growth in population which led to a demand for a larger church independent of Jarrow. In 1784 the Rev. Richard Wallis got permission to enlarge the church and extensive alterations were made in 1810 in a successful effort to support the sagging roof. In 1845 St Hild's became independent. In 1941 much damage was done to the church during a bombing raid but in 1949 it was restored and in 1977 it was beautifully redecorated.

The model lifeboat suspended from the nave ceiling is a replica of the first lifeboat to be built in Britain and when South Shields was made a Municipal Borough in 1851 the lifeboat was incorporated into his coats of arms. Its motto is Always Ready.

The designer of the first lifeboat certainly came from South Shields but who was he? Was it William Wouldhave (1751-1824) or was it Henry Greathead (1757-1816). Let us compromise and credit both men with the idea following the tragedy of the Newcastle brig *Adventure* which was driven ashore at South Shields and eight crew died with the South Shields folk watching but unable to act. Something had to be done and a life boat was suggested In 1789 a boat called the *Original* was launched and both Greathead and Wouldhave were involved. The Lifeboat memorial close to the South Shields shore was built to celebrate Queen Victoria's Jubilee in 1887. On display, protected by a canopy and an iron barrier is the lifeboat *Tyne* which operated between 1833 and 1894. It differs very little from the *Original*, was built by J. Oliver of South Shields and is now Britain's second oldest preserved lifeboat.

Down from the lifeboat memorial is a typical resort beach with ice cream, fish and chip, and hamburger stalls and all set around good flat soft sand. These days the waters of the Tyne estuary are much cleaner and bathing is becoming ever more popular. Few beaches have a more beautiful backdrop and across the river is Tynemouth Priory. This is seen even better from the high land above Arbeia fort and close to the Beacon and Harbour Lights Hotels both of which serve excellent meals. Across from the hotels are a couple of cannons, pointing over the harbour and South Shields beaches to North Shields. Here are two structures called the Lawe Beacons, one situated between the two hotels and the other right on the headland. The latter has been well preserved. It was erected in 1832 by John Turnbull to replace 18th century structures and at a cost of £60. They were meant to work as navigational aids in conjunction with the High and Low lights at North Shields.

Like any seaside town South Shields has an inspiring waterfront especially in the Mill Dam area which has been recently restored and was used by Catherine Cookson in her novels Colour Blind and the Tide of Life series. Inns like the Steamboat have their tales to tell and it is said that it has a resident ghost. This may be fictional but it is a fact that drunken men were taken from the Steamboat to boats moored at the mill dam. Also worth searching out are the statues of Dolly Peel and the Man with the Donkey. Dolly died at the age of 75 in 1857 having lived a very active life and earning a healthy living as a notorious smuggler although her legitimate trade was supposed to be that of a fishwife. She was also popular with local sailors and was said to have sheltered men from the Press Gang beneath her petticoats. Dolly was a woman of great intelligence and in her own way a person of great courage. Another hero was the man with the donkey. He was John Simpson Kirkpatrick born on South Eldon Street in 1897 and who showed his courage during the ill-fated Gallipoli. John emigrated to Australia but then joined the Anzak forces and found himself fighting in the Balkans with his friends being shot all around him. He threw away his rifle and used a donkey which he called Murphy and the pair ferried the wounded back to safety. Later John Kirkpatrick was killed and is a national hero in Australia but is also commemorated in his native town by the statue with his donkey. During the Second World War, South Shields produced its share of heroes and more than 3000 local seamen died and in 1990 the Countess Mountbatten of Burma unveiled a memorial to them at Mill Dam.

These days South Shields and district is dominated by Catherine Cookson and plaques mark locations used in her novels whilst discovery trips are organised by coach into the more distant locations. In the South Shields Museum and Art Gallery there is an area devoted to her life. The facade of William Black Street in East Jarrow where Catherine spent much of her childhood has been reconstructed. The designers have been helped by reference to her autobiography Our Kate and have recreated Cissie Affleck's sweet shop and the kitchen of her house. This is not just an appreciation of an important author but a social history lesson.

Although removed from Durham in 1974, South Shields is still to us part of the County of the Prince Bishops. It has a

The South Shields ferry across to North Shields runs regularly from the Market Place Quay.

special place in our affections as South Shields was the birthplace of one of our grandmothers. We never tired of listening to her accent and stories of the glories of shipbuilding along the Tyne which was the old border between Northumberland and Durham. She told us of Jarrow, the march and the Venerable Bede and of the skills of the warship builders at Hebbern. She also told us of her seaman father going down to the Mill Dam in search of work and how granddad also sailed out of the port at the time they were courting in the late 1890s. This dam took its name from the large corn mill which once stood on a water inlet and which was filled in during 1819 to provide an occupation for soldiers left idle at the end of the Napoleonic wars. It soon developed into a meeting point for seamen and around the Mill Dam there developed chandlers, pubs, a customs' house, Port Health Authority building and a launching ramp. From 1960 little use was made of the area and by the late 1970s the Mill Dam area was derelict, but in the last few years it has been sensitively restored and brings back a feeling of the halcyon days of sail.

The lifeboat memorial at South Shields.

An even earlier time of Durham dominance can be found at Jarrow, the birthplace of Anglo-Saxon religious culture. Even though it was initiated from Monkwearmouth it is Jarrow which is the more famous.

Jarrow, once a shipbuilding area famous in the annals of the Royal Navy, fell on hard times after the First World War and in 1936 the famous Jarrow Marchers walked to London to draw attention to their plight. The workers of Jarrow were well known to Catherine Cookson and many of her books are based in and around the town. Reading of its industrial history we were surprised when our grandmother described the beauties of the area.

The Christian heritage of Jarrow is still very evident despite the fact that the old church and even older monastery are surrounded by industry and a forest of electric pylons. There is ample parking between St Paul's church and the Jarrow Slake which is a minor tributary to the Tyne.

The Anglo-Saxon monastery was founded in AD 681 by Benedict Biscop and had it not been for one of its monks Jarrow would just have been another little house decimated by the Vikings. St Paul's monastery was the base of one of the most remarkable scholars of Europe - the truly Venerable Bede speculated that the world was round 'not like a dish, but like a sphere'. He also wrote A History of the English Church and People without travelling any distance from Jarrow.

Bede entered the Monastery of St Peter's in 680 and it is thought that what is now the parish church was dedicated at the same time. It may originally have been the Saxon chapel of St Mary. Bede himself wrote more than 60 works and so he is quite able to write his own biography in words which ring out through the ages. Bede died in his cell at Jarrow on Ascension Eve AD 735.

'I was born on the lands of this monastery, and on reaching seven years of age, I was entrusted by my family first to the Most Reverend Abbot Benedict and later to Abbot Ceolfrith for my education. I have spent all the remainder of my life in this monastery and devoted myself entirely to the study of the Scriptures. And while I have observed the regular discipline and sung the choir offices daily in church, my chief delight has always been in study, teaching and writing. I was ordained deacon in my nineteenth year, and priest in my thirtieth, receiving both these orders at the hands of the Most Reverend Bishop John at the direction of Abbot Coelfrith. From the time of my receiving the priesthood until my fifty-ninth year, I have worked, both for my own benefit and that of my brethren, to compile short extracts from the works of the Venerable Fathers on Holy Scripture and to comment on their meaning and interpretation.'

Along with those of Cuthbert Bede's bones did not rest in peace but were subjected to a reluctant journey before coming to rest at Durham. In AD 73 he was buried at the west end of Jarrow church but his bones were stolen in 1020 by Alfred Westou one of Durham's clerics and placed with those of Cuthbert. No doubt this was meant as a compliment to Bede's greatness but it would have been more Christian to leave him in his beloved Jarrow. Bede's bones are now in the Galilee chapel of Durham Cathedral.

Battery Point at South Shields looking across the Tyne to North Shields and Tynemouth.

Long before the bones of Bede were stolen, the monastery fell on hard times and was sacked by the Vikings in AD 794 along with many others along the North East coast. There is evidence that fire destroyed at least some of the old buildings, but what was not destroyed was the knowledge spread by the writings of the venerable Bede. It was these writings which in 1072 resulted in the Benedictines re-occupying the ancient site of learning in reverence to Bede. Aldwin the Prior of Winchcombe in Gloucestershire accompanied by monks from Evesham visited the site and encouraged by Bishop Walcher of Durham the new buildings were commenced. Apart from the bones of Bede which had been removed to Durham some remnants of the original monastery can be found in the sanctuary of the present Monastic Parish Church of St. Paul.

On entering this church the visitor is given an immediate surprise. From the outside it looks to be a neglected church set deep in an industrial setting. Inside, however, is a well stocked shop and a warm welcome from the parishioners who provide an informative guide service. Saxon remains

The church at Jarrow seen through the ruined walls of the medieval monastery.

include Bede's chair, an aumbry, the Jarrow cross, the Dedication stone, the Baluster frieze and shafts. The chair is indeed ancient, but did it once belong to the Venerable Bede? Scientists have applied carbon 14 dating techniques to a small splinter taken from the chair and has been dated to around 1,100 years ago. It could therefore have been part of Bede's furniture.

The aumbrey is still used as a cupboard to hold the vessels used for the Eucharist just as it was in the Saxon monastery when Holy Mass was celebrated. It is one of the best preserved Saxon aumbreys. The Dedication stone of the original monastery still survives and is seen over the western arch of the church tower. The inscription is in Latin but translates as follows:

The dedication of the church of St Paul on 23rd April in the fifteenth year of King Ecgfrith and the fourth year Ceolfrith Abbot and under God's guidance founder of this same church.

Detail of the Jarrow Cross.

Ecgfrith ascended the throne in AD 670 and thus we know
that the monastery was founded in 685. The Jarrow cross
may well be of the same period, but a piece of Roman stone
was used in its construction. The cross was discovered in
1866 when the present nave was under construction. Much
of interest remains even though the head is missing and the
arms are now detached and kept in the museum of antiquities
across the Tyne at Newcastle. The inscription which is still
legible translates from the Latin as 'In this unique sign life

The River Tyne photographed from the picnic site at Heddon.

is restored to the world' and both this and the cross are in the logo adopted by the Jarrow parish. The cross is probably contemporary with the Dedication stone and some scholars believe that the writing refers to Constantine, the first Christian Emperor of Rome, and his vision of the cross before the battle of Mulvain Bridge in AD 312. This is described in Rufinus's translation of the Ecclesiastical History written by Eusabius. A copy of this was in the Jarrow monastery library and was read by Bede and incorporated into his writings. During the church reconstructions of 1782 many 7th and 8th century stones were re-used in the new church and the Baluster frieze and shaft date to this period. This re-use of existing stone was not new and the chancel first built in AD 581 used Roman masonry taken from either Hadrian's wall at Wallsend or from the South Shields fort of Arbeia.

Some remnants also remain of the medieval church including some particularly fine choir stalls and a couple of bells. The dark oak choir stalls date to the time of Thomas Castell, Prior of Durham from 1495 to 1519, but other stalls in the south of the chancel are early Victorian copies, but very skilful work nevertheless.

Jarrow has two bells which are among the oldest in England the tenor dating to the 13th century and the treble about a century later. The sound of these would have been known to the Jarrow monks long before the Reformation. St Paul's was suppressed in 1536 at the very beginning of the Reformation, a sure sign that the house was only small because the less influential houses were suppressed first. Although most of the Jarrow buildings were dismantled the church was left standing to serve as the parish church. The parish records date from 1572 but in 1710 the rector moved to Heworth and from which he controlled a huge parish stretching from Felling to South Shields. Jarrow church was not abandoned, however, but was so neglected by 1782 that substantial reconstruction was needed. The subsequent industrial growth of Jarrow based upon mining and shipbuilding led to a return of the rector.

Just opposite the church is a pleasant park, above which is the Bede Monastery Museum, also an important place of pilgrimage for Anglo-Saxon and ecclesiastical scholars. This and the monastery itself is signposted from the A185 near the Tyne Tunnel and there is a small entry fee. Between April and October it opens from Tuesday to Saturday from 10 am to 5.30 pm and on Sundays between 10 am and 5.30 pm. In winter the Sunday opening hours are the same but it opens from Tuesday to Saturday between 11 am and 4.30 pm. Apart from Bank Holidays the museum closes on Mondays.

The museum houses many artefacts recovered during excavations of the monastery and included are bits of Saxon window glass, among the oldest to be found in England. There is a model of the monastery as it would have appeared in the 8th century along with an audio visual presentation of the life of a monk which was by no means easy. The day was one of almost continual prayer beginning with Vigil or Matins at 2 am, followed by Lauds at 5 am, Prime at 6.30 am, Terce at 8.15 am, Sext at midday, None at 2.30 pm, Vespers at 4.15 pm and finally Compline at 5 pm. Between this strict schedule Bede and his fellow monks had to find time to study, attend to their ablutions and to eat.

The Bede Monastery Museum has lots of exhibits including Anglo-Saxon and Celtic displays plus a medieval room. There is also an Information Centre, a shop, herb garden and a cafe. The building itself - Jarrow Hall - is an

interesting building in its own right. It was built in 1800 built
for a wealthy industrialist named Simon Temple. It was used
as Mary Llewellyn's house in the television adaptation of
Catherine Cookson's novel The Fifteenth Streets.

On the opposite side of the main South Shields road is the
Bede Gallery close to Springwell Park and surrounded by a
housing estate. The gallery is a most unattractive building
but is of interest to those fascinated by Jarrow's history or
modern art and entry is free. Here is told the story of the
Jarrow march of 1936 led by their formidable lady MP Helen
Wilkinson. The historic and courageous event is commemorated by a plaque at the entrance of the Town Hall. In the
modern shopping precinct is a statue commemorating the
Viking raids which took place in AD 793 and 796. More
modern battles take place on the athletics track at Monkton
Stadium situated close to the Bede Gallery. This has been
the training ground for many famous athletes including
Steve Cram and David Sharpe.

Around Jarrow and nearby Heddon are a number of
extensive riverside walks created by very intelligent landscaping from what were old docks and shipbuilding yards.
Not all these have gone and one area between Jarrow and
Heddon would make a magnificent maritime museum. A
half-hearted effort, no doubt strangled by lack of money, has
been made to restore HMS *Cavalier* berthed at the former
Hawthorn Leslie Shipyard. Alas this Second World War
destroyer is not yet open to the public and is rather difficult
to view through the closed dock gates.

No tourist should ever write off Hebburn as an industrial
wasteland. Although it is still centred around the Swan
Hunter Shipyards which once built some of Britain's most
powerful warships, it has now been slimmed down
modernised, and its environment improved. As we were
putting the finishing touches to this manuscript in the late
summer of 1993 Swan Hunter announced yet more job losses
in a further effort to stay in business and maintain its long
and distinguished history.

On the southern bank of the Tyne almost all the industrial
clutter has either been removed or buried beneath the skilful
landscaping which has produced a most attractive riverside

park with plenty of parking and grassy banks on which to picnic. On the river itself a line of pleasure craft lie at anchor opposite the brightly coloured cranes and we watched a dredger removing silt from the bed of the Tyne and thus keeping the channel open on the way up-stream to Newcastle. We watched terns diving for food and a cormorant riding on the current as the tide pushed its way up the Tyne.

Despite the boundary changes of 1974 we still feel that the Tyne is the true boundary between the counties of Durham and Northumberland. The latter is the subject of our companion volume published in this series in 1992.

Further Reading

Durham County Council (1980) The Durham Book (Durham C. C.)

Ekwall, E. (1960) The Concise Oxford Dictionary of English Place Names (Oxford Clarendon Press)

Fraser, C. and Emsley, K. (1978) Northumbria (Batsford)

Freethy, Ron and Marlene (1992) Discovering Northumberland (John Donald)

Freethy, Ron and Marlene (1992) Discovering the Pennines (John Donald)

Green, Dudley (1992) Discovering Hadrian's Wall (John Donald)

Grierson, E. (1976) Companion Guide to Northumbria (Collins)

Heavisides, M. (1989) Rambles by the River Tees (Rigg)

Hillery, C. and Parker, M. (1990) Durham City and County (Discovery Guides)

Johnson, M. (1987) Durham Historic and University City (Turnstone)

Le Guillou, M. (1978) A History of the River Tees (Cleveland County Libraries)

Mee, A. (Ed) (1960) The King's England - Durham (Hodder & Stoughton)

Ordnance Survey (1987) Leisure Guide - Northumbria (The A.A.)

Pevsner, N. (1953) The Buildings of England - Durham (Penguin)

Ramsden, D. M. (1947) Teesdale (Museum Press)

Selkirk, R. (1975) The Piercebridge Formula (Stephens)

Spencer, B. (1988) The Shell Guide to North East England (Michael Joseph)

Tallentire, W. (1988) Middleton-in-Teesdale (Discovery Guide)

Thorold, H. (1980) County Durham (Faber & Faber)

Tomlin, D. M. (1975) Teeside's Economic Heritage (Cleveland County Council)

Watson, R. (1930) Poems and Songs of Teesdale (Dresser)

Wedgewood, I. (1932) Northumberland and Durham (Faber & Faber)

Woodhouse, R. (1991) The River Tees. (Terence Dalton)

Index